Spir

MW00936545

Spirit Of Bilal
The Community Is Born

Spirit Of Bilal
The Community Is Born

Calling The World
To Human Excellence

By
IMAM SHAHID ABDULLAH

Foreword by Laila Muhammad

Spirit Of Bilal: The Community Is Born

2018 First Edition

By Shahid Abdullah

www.shahidabdullah.com

First printing 2018

Printed in the United States
Editors: Gail Muhammad
          Aisha T. Toure
Cover Design: Imam Shahid Abdullah (Cen. IMAM W. DEEN MOHAMMED, Lt. Imam Mustafah El-Amin, Rt. Akbar Salaam)
Foreword: Laila Muhammad
Order inquiries: shahid_abdullah2000@yahoo.com or www.shahidabdullah.com

Spirit of Bilal

DEDICATION AND APPRECIATION

This book is in dedication to Imam W. D. Mohammed for his enormous effort and achievement in completing a mission that was second only to the great prophets and Muhammad Ibn Abdullah, the Messenger of Allah (PBUH).

It is also with great appreciation I thank Allah for The Honorable Elijah Muhammad and Fard Muhammad. Their work was immeasurable as to the value and the sacrifices they made for this community to be born.

With admiration and gratitude, I thank all the African Slaves who were brought to America on the ships that delivered them to a life of torment with little to no relief from anguish inflicted on them by Slave Master on the plantations in the Americas. They suffered the backbreaking life of growing rice, picking cotton and tobacco to furnish Europeans and Caucasian-Americans with raw products necessary to usher in the industrial age in the west.

I thank the African-American people such as George Washington Carver, Booker T. Washington, Fredrick Douglas, Benjamin Banneker, Sojourner Truth, Mary Bethune Cookman, Shirley Chisholm, Clara Muhammad, Dr. Martin Luther King, Jr., and hundreds of other men and women for enduring segregation, racism, police brutality, deadly, family-destroying drugs introduced to our community by members of the Caucasian-American community; the last hired and first fired policy and all the other policies and actions that deprived the African-American people of the opportunity of an honorable life in America.

Most of all, I thank Allah for delivering us out of that inhuman and unjust condition. I thank Him for His Mercy by raising us from the bottom of civilization.

TABLE OF CONTENT

FOREWORD: *"Spirit Of Bilal"*

As the daughter of Imam W. D. Mohammed (RA) and the grand-daughter of The Honorable Elijah Muhammad (RA), I'm pleased and filled with elation as to the powerful message conveyed in Spirit of Bilal. It captures their mission in a very straight forward and detailed approach as to their roles in our history.

My father's life began as one who would help his father to uplift the Blackman in America; subsequently it evolved into a life that produced a new community that would call the world to human excellence.

I recall him saying, "Life is serious business Laila, and we must live the words of the Adhan— Come To Cultivation; Come To Success."

Spirit of Bilal will empower you with answers to many of your questions; you may even find new questions coming to life. Simultaneous, the logic being followed and the natural conclusion being reached, will stimulate your intellect as it warms your heart. It will support and evolve your independent rational thinking as a human being.

Page after page, you will travel a thought provoking and intellectually stimulating journey. At the end of this journey, you will hear the voice of freedom echoing through time.

Laila Muhammad,
April 15, 2018

INTRODUCTION

There are few events in the history of mankind that affect humanity as much as this new community born out of the African-American experience in America. It is the guiding light calling the world to Human Excellence—having the moral courage to be morally upright, truth in life, unselfish, charitable, want to help the members of the society, and feel the burdens of the sins and the problems of the whole society.

Taking to the air, the development of the era of information with the computer and the harnessing of electrical power are all moments in our history that linked and shaped our civilization. These are defining moments that bond us; they bring us closer to spiritual oneness.

Similarly, there are social events that have the same or even more of an impact on our pursuit of life. One such event is the birth of this community.

The history of the African-American people shows many interesting and varied paths journeyed by a people lost in a cultural maze induced by unavoidable historical events. As descendents from Africa whose original cultures were striped as a result of their enslavement in America, they began their journey as free people without a complete knowledge of their common language, religion and interest. The absence of these valuable qualities that are necessary for community life, are the aspects that a culture gives to its people. This absence left them as a people blinded by the lack of hindsight to assist them in the task of creating a positive future.

Formed in time and shaped by global circumstances, a special community could only come into existence by the Mercy of Allah. Their spiritual eyes, as the majority of the world, were covered by superstitions, symbolic languages and religious ignorance that hovered over the world of knowledge like an enormous black cloud that blocked the light of understanding from the conscious mind.

This challenge gave birth to a new community that encourages the world to go all-out on the path of Human Excellence to develop Moral Leadership in the society for Human Salvation.

While engaging your religious belief, this book will challenge your understanding by broadening your vision of religious history and its impact in the modern world. How the human beings came into religious life and why, are the questions that are answered in a clear and comprehensive approach thus giving birth to a new insight.

The history of this community will amaze you as you trace its emergences on the world stage in the role of a voice for Human Salvation—an achievement that is only found in Biblical and Qur'anic rationalization. Hidden in symbolic language, communicating beautiful concepts defined in religious scripture over a thousand years ago, it is the prophetic realization of these concepts that manifest in the form of a miracle.

In the language of the Qur'an, Allah makes it clear that He will raise a community with the spirit of Al-Islam to call the world to Human Excellence. In this modern era, the community that fills this prophetic description the best was formed in America. It was created from the African-American experience because it was the picture of adversities and suffering; it was the foundation that enabled them to be guided by the moral fiber in the human soul. The spirit that Allah intended to come into the human heart has been resurrected in this community to mirror the character of the original community of peace established by Prophet Muhammed Ibn Abdullah (PBUH) 1400 years ago.

The original community was an example for humanity to live in peace, and the importance of moral leadership in every human being. However, over the years, its ideal character was buried under the drifting sands of human error. For generations, many signs have appeared and pointed to this phenomenon and its rebirth in the form of a new community. The strongest of these signs is connected with the man called Bilal. He exemplified loyalty and dedication to Prophet Muhammed and the principles and value of that original community. In essence, this new community born in this present time will point the world to Human Excellence by calling to them with the same spirit of a servant of Allah, Bilal Ibn Rabah.

CHAPTER 1

SEEING IS BELIEVING

Bilal the voice of freedom was an Ethiopian born in Mecca in the late 6th century, sometime between 578 and 582. He displayed the spirit of loyalty and dedication to Prophet Muhammad Ibn Abdullah (PBUH) and the message of Al-Islam that would be the corner stone of the community. Additionally, he was the first Mu'adhan (The one who calls the Muslim community to come together and pray in unity). The call to prayer started more than 1,400 years ago, as the Prophet received the order from Allah to have the worshippers the devotees of Al-Islam to start conducting prayers.

According to the Hadith (narrations of sayings and actions of the accounts of The Prophet) by Bukhari, after leaving Makkah and migrating to Madinah, the number of Muslims started to increase. Prophet Muhammad built Masjid Al-Nabawi to offer Salaah regularly. The people announced in a loud voice. **"As-salat ul-jamiah (the Salaah for jama'ah is ready)."** Those who heard this call came to join the Salaah (prayer). The Prophet asked his devoted companions for their advice as to how the calls should be made.

Some of them suggested that the Muslims, like the Jews, should blow a horn to announce the time for the prayer. Others said that they should ring bells as the Christians. Still other proposed to kindle a fire like the fire-worshippers. However, Prophet Muhammad wasn't satisfied with any of these ideas.

One day, a companion, Abdullah ibn Zaid came to him and said, "O Messenger of Allah! I had a beautiful dream last night."

After the Prophet inquired about the dream, Zaid said, "I've seen that a man wearing green garment taught me the words of the Adhan and advised me to call people to prayer with these words." He then recited these words, ***"Allahu Akbar, Allahu Akbar (***God is great***); Ash hadu anna la elaha ella Allah [repeated] (***I testify that there is no god but Allah***); Ash hadu anna muhammadan rasulo Allah (***I testify that Muhammed is Allah's messenger***); Hayya Ala alSallah (***Come to prayer***); Hayya Ala alFallah (***Come to success***); Allahu Akbar (***God is great***);***

La Elaha Ella Allah (There is no god but Allah***).***
The words were beautiful and full of meaning. In addition to Zaid, Umar ibn Khatib was one of the persons who came and said: "O Messenger of Allah, an

angel taught me the same words in my dream last night."

After recognizing that the dream of Zaid was true, the Prophet accepted this Adhan as the official call to the prayer. He then asked Zaid to teach the words of Adhan to Bilal.

It was well known throughout the Muslim community that Bilal had a beautiful and strong voice. Shortly afterward, Bilal stood up and called the Adhan. The voice of Bilal resounded throughout Madinah. People came running to Masjid Al-Nabawi.

Many years after *Bukhari's Hadith,* as one of the tradition in Al-Islam, the Adhan is practiced throughout the Muslim world today as it was established by the Prophet, and next to him, Bilal stands as a most important figure in connection with the Adhan—the sign that defines humanity was one family. Astonishingly, as one of the most prominent figures in Islamic history, Bilal began as a slave and rose to become the minister of finance and treasurer-general for Prophet Muhammed.

Although his full name was Bilal ibn Rabah, he was sometimes called Bilal al-Habashi (Bilal the Ethiopian). He was bushy haired, tall, dark and known to have a beautiful voice. He was exceptionally close to the Prophet, and was a model of steadfastness and devotion to the faith.

His dedication remains a classic and frequently cited story in that he suffered for his immediate acceptance of the message of Al-Islam from Prophet Muhammed. The story pointed out that Bilal accepted Al-Islam while he was still a slave. As a slave, his master, Umayya ibn Khalaf reportedly, "would bring him out at the hottest part of the day and throw him on his back in the open valley and have a great rock put on his chest; then he would say to him, 'You will stay here till you die or deny Muhammed and worship al-Lat and al-'Uzza" (pre-Islamic goddesses). Bilal's loyalty to Prophet Muhammed and the faith he taught began as a matter of life or death. Of course, he never renounced The Prophet or the message he brought. Subsequently, his freedom was bought by Abu Bakr, a companion of the Prophet Muhammed. He was freed to follow Allah's word as conveyed and practiced by the Prophet without restrictions and the domination of anyone.

His loyalty is a reminder that in the Prophet's eyes, the measure of a man was neither nationality nor social status, but piety. It is stated in Bukhari Hadith that The

Spirit of Bilal

Prophet said to Bilal, "I heard the sound of your shoes in Paradise just in front of me."

The Spirit of Human Excellence in Bilal was recognized by many; it is also reported that the Shi'a Imam Ja'far said, "May God bless Bilal! He loved us, the family of Muhammed, and was one of most pious servants of God." In terms of commitment and dedication, it was stated that Bilal alone was worth a third of all Islam.

On an occasion regarded as one of the most hallowed moments in Islamic history, after the Muslim forces had captured Mecca, Bilal ascended to the top of the Ka'ba to call the believers to prayer. This was the first time the call to prayer was heard within Islam's holiest city.

It is very easy to understand why our beloved Imam W. D. Mohammed, on November 7, 1975, chose for the African-American people the name "Bilalian" as an ethic identity. The impact that Bilal had on Islamic history was extra special. Imam Mohammed acknowledged Bilal as a spiritual and ethnic representative; he suggested that the African-American Muslim community had a direct connection and should identify themselves with him.

However, in keeping with his objective and to avoid the idea that he was starting a new sect of Al-Islam in America, Imam Mohammed stopped the use of Bilalian as a group identity; he did not want to draw attention away from his message; he wanted to make sure that the significance of his core message was clear without any unnecessary confusion.

This did not diminish the importance of Bilal; in fact, it brought our attention to the spirit exemplified in Bilal. It was the spirit of steadfastness and devotion to the faith established by Prophet Muhammed.

CHAPTER 2

UNCOMPROMISING

The exemplary community formed 1400 years ago in the mist of the Arabian Desert by Prophet Muhammed did not just suddenly spring up in history out of insignificance. It can be traced back to the humble beginning of human existence on this planet; it evolved purposefully from the dust of the earth.

In the Holy Qur'an, Allah uses Balance Ummah to define the community life that flourishes on the basis of peace as an example to humanity to bring about peace in the society of the secular world. Not just any Ummah, but one that is not given to extremes. It is led by the Moral Conscience striving for Human Excellence.

In Surah Baqarah, Ayah 143, Allah says, "Thus have We made of you an Ummah justly balanced that ye might be witnesses over the nations and the Apostle a witness over yourselves; and We appointed the Qiblah to which thou wast used only to test those who followed the Apostle from those who would turn on their heels (from the faith). Indeed, it was (a change) momentous except to those guided by Allah. And never would Allah make your faith of no effect. For Allah is to all people most surely full of kindness Most Merciful." Understanding this Ayah begins with the concept of Ummah.

Ummah is the word that Allah uses in the Holy Qur'an that means community in English; it is rooted in the term Ummi (the Arabic word for mother). Allah says in the women He puts life, and she is to guard and nourish that life. She is life and the environment for life: like culture, Ummah comes from this concept. This suggests to us that an Ummah is a social group that perpetuates certain characteristics that identifies it, and it is the environment that supports life. This is beyond the existence that only requires the acquisition and distribution of food, clothing and shelter which are needs of the individual as well as the group. The Ummah is a way of life, formation and survival that depends on the subtleties of its common interest such as language, religion, economics, education or ideology.

The connection between the ideal position and perceived reality can be made as recorded history emerges with scriptural interpretations as it relates to this special Ummah.

"Thus have We made of you an Ummah justly balanced..." This portion of the Ayah indicates the evolution of the human being is a long term relationship that mankind has had with Allah. The human being is a social creature. Ummah is addressing the social life while respecting the sovereignty of the individual; it brings our attention to individuals co-existing. Like all scripture, Ayah 143 must be evaluated on the basis of its position in history.

In the phrase "We made of you…" are two positions; one is the evolution of mankind; and the other points out that different components were put together to form the right community. It draws our attention to the fact that we had been shaped by the circumstance over time that defines us historically as a creature that was shaped by something other than our own abilities. Even the way we understand religion was a process that grew over time.

Many scholars and historians agree that the history of religion in mankind can be traced back to our early beginning. Mankind's connection with religion is a fact in history that describes our primitive or official basis and formation of our devotion to a deity. This development took thousands of years; from an elementary beginning, right up until the conclusion in the time of Prophet Muhammed.

While historians recorded the events, the Bible gives a good account also, but its account is incomplete because it suggests that one will to bring the people into all truth. Perhaps the most complete and best account is found in the Holy Qur'an. The problem that most people have with either account is in understanding the picture language found in the revealed text. However, thanks to the language Allah blessed Imam W. D. Mohammed with; we can understand this picture language of religious text by applying our rational mind, and following a concept to its logical conclusion.

We begin this thought with the Bible where it says, "All in the first Adam will die and all in the second Adam will live..." This picture is illustrated in both Holy Qur'an and Bible that suggest a way thinking or viewing life that had to evolve.

Early human beings contended with and tried to understand the creation with their emotions, urges and impulses. They had only evolved emotionally; and that state was not enough to guarantee our species. We could not contend with the wild animals and terrain of that ancient world; we were not physically equipped to deal with that harsh environment. Had it not been for our ability to reason or use our rational mind, we would have perished along with our friend the dinosaur and became a relic. Praise be to Allah, there came a time in our ancient history that the rational ability that Allah created in the human being began to separate us from the beast of the fields. We were no longer depending on just our emotional capacity such as fear to protect us from harm. We had evolved to use our intellect as our primary approach to the creation. Our intellect was formed from our sense of sight, taste, sound, touch and smell as the building block of our rational mind.

These five senses are the package that the Creator gave us to receive the bits and pieces of information in our mind from the physical world. This information would stimulate our mind to serve our imagination which marked the beginning of civilization on earth. The secular world we see today came into existence from this elementary start.

Simultaneously, these same five senses were used to develop our early understanding of a deity; another part of Allah's Plan had begun to unfold; the dawn of the religious community that would guide the secular world.

Spirit of Bilal

CHAPTER 3

FAVORING ITS EXISTENCE

The scripture says that Allah found favor in Noah. He was a friend to Allah; he even walked with Him, according to some scriptures. More important, he, his family, the era and the ark were the early symbols that require interpretation in order to comprehend the first encounter in and the chain that links in our religious history.

Noah, in scripture, does not merely represent an individual as much as he does a community that began to reason with its existence. Thousands of years ago, the foundation for the future of human history was being laid—a history that included our perception about the existence of a deity and its involvement in human life.

Religious scriptures suggest that not only were the five senses (sight, hear, taste, touch and smell) used for survival in the physical world that surrounded early man, but they are also symbolic of Noah and his family. Combined with the events of that time, which also are symbols with a greater meaning, Noah is symbolic to the sense of sight in the human being because he was

27

the first to recognize the existence of a deity. In other words, when the human being began to recognize the G-d, that period is symbolized by the name Noah. The rest of his family represents the other four senses in the human being.

For example, Noah is one, his wife is another and his three surviving sons represent the other four senses. However, in the story of Noah, some religious text suggests and states that Noah's sons had wives, and that one or a fourth son drowned or was overcome by the waters — leaving some scholars to question the number of sons that Noah had. Not to damping this argument, it is more important recognizing how the story of Noah fit into human history. In other words, symbolically, Noah and his family represent our five senses that exist in every human being, and what part the senses played in our evolutionary process. Furthermore, primitive man evolved in their understanding or search for a deity in the same manner. It paralleled the story of Noah.

They approached their concept of a deity as though the deity was part of the creation. More important, the use of rational thinking had become their process for understanding religion as in Ancient Egypt (Kemet). Following this train of thought, to gain a better understanding, we must unravel the symbolism in story of Noah, the Ark and the animals by interpreting the picture presented in scripture.

The Ark represented the religious insight of the human being as they evolved into a community. It also signals the beginning of correct worship. This aspect of human life is the separation of the religious community from the direction of development of the secular society. Historians describe this period as a form of worship; this appears to be connected to the term Ark. An ark is a ship or very large boat. Ironically, in the historian's word, worship is the word "ship." This is more than coincidence because the Ark is a ship. Furthermore, in the language of Imam Mohammed, he referred to the ark as a form of worship. Theoretically, they both carry the passengers to safety.

The Ark represents the world of human beings coming into a religious community byway of this rational approach. It was the embryo which saved this early religious community from the pitfalls of the secular society. As the story continues, the water that drowned the people represented the end of that old approach to relating to the creation, and the beginning of direct guidance from the Creator.

Water is the symbol for emotions and human sentiments. The primitive instincts had to give way to the rational mind; the time had come for the human beings to be more rational in their ascension into the community life that was planned by Allah.

The animals in the Ark represented the primitive ways such urges, impulses and influence that stayed with the human being right down to these modern times; but, they had to remain under the control or the authority of the conscious mind byway of the Moral Conscience.

Urges are part of our emotional nature (the Jinn). An urge is a force or impulse within us that compels us to put into motion an action of progression or regression with energy and enthusiasm. Simply put, for example, eating is a necessary function the body must perform in order to survive. To encourage the process of eating, hunger is linked to the emotions of which urge is a part; urge is the force that triggers the mind to take in food for human survival.

On the other hand, influence is the power or capacity of causing an effect in direct or intangible ways. Religious scripture refers to this capacity as clay or mud fashioned into shape because it reacts or responds to internal as well as external suggestions, hints or clues. There are good influences and bad ones.

For example, a good influence was the affect that birds flying had on of our will to fly. This was a hint to humans; it was their flight that influenced our desire to build airplanes as a primary form of transportation. On the other hand, influence can also cause harm to our character.

Influence is the one characteristic of the human being that makes us susceptible or vulnerable to wrong doing or sinning. It is the area that Satan tries to suggest or call the human being away from Allah. To accomplish this, Satan uses temptation as a force of influence. Temptation is the force of inducement; the enticement to do wrong by promise of pleasure or gain.

In his last sermon, Prophet Muhammed (PBUH) warns us as he stated, "Beware of Satan, for your safety of your religion. He has lost all hope that he will ever be able to lead you astray in big things, so beware of following him in small things." While this is a direct warning, it suggests that the control is in our hands.

Urges and influences can be checked by the intellect or Moral Conscience. For example, fasting can check the urge to eat; and, according to Qur'an, it also checks temptation by teaching self-restraint. Urges and influences are some of the primeval ways; the ways or forces that were with humans in their earliest stage.

When modern humans allow these urges or temptations to be first to drive their actions, they are in a primeval state or primitive mode and easily directed by Satan. Nevertheless, these primitive instincts are valuable because they receive the good suggestions and hints that are all around us. They are in the form of signs in the creature that hint or suggest to us Allah's plan. They have been a guide for the human being from their beginning.

As early man began to use fire, make weapons and discover the many things that the creation surrendered up to them, they built their world out of the surrounding material they found in the earth. This included his concept of a deity that they made from stone. This was followed by the sacrifice of human life as a way to please the deity.

CHAPTER 4

ELEVATING THE MIND

While using their rational mind the community evolved to the next level of understanding. This level was given the name Ibrahiim or Abraham. In the picture language of the scripture, it says that Ibrahiim told his father that the deities they were worshipping were not the Creator. The term father in this picture represents a philosophical generation of the past...the generation of Noah which evolved into polytheism and the worship of images (Ibrahiim's father).

The Abraham generation signals the level of thinking when human beings became conscious of the fact that while they were learning and receiving signs from the creation, the creation was not the Creator; their G-d was greater then the Creation. And, most important, the community established that the Creator is One with no associates. While historians may not verify the existence of Abraham, they do agree about the arrival of the concept of monotheism (the Belief in One G-d).

In fact, during the period between 1375 and 1358 B.C., history records that a pharaoh named Akhenaten (Amenhotep IV) attempted to bring the concept of one

G-d to Ancient Egypt as the base belief. While history does not depict the source of his inspiration, it does state that he changed his name to Akhenaten which meant "Glory to Aten." This phrase is very similar to the Christian who says, "Glory to G-d" and the Muslim who says "Al Hamdulillah" or "All Praise is Due to Allah".

Akhenaten ordered the images of Amon and the lesser gods to be removed from all public places and monuments; Aten was supreme and the only G-d. According to Ninian Smart, author of The Religious Experience of Mankind, on page 222, these are words Akhenaten used while addressing his Lord: "How numerous are Thy works, they are concealed from the vision of men, O sole God, other than whom there is no other. Thou hast created the earth according to thy heart, with men and flocks and all the animals ...Thou dost apportion to each man his place, thou provideth for his needs: each has his nourishment, and the hour of his death is fixed...." This rendition fastens the connection between the theory and fact of monotheism. However, after Akhenaten passed, Egypt converted back to polytheism or the belief in many G-ds.

Another important factor concerning Abraham's generation was that it also concluded a period of sacrificing a living human being to a deity in the name of religion. This was illustrated when Ibrahim, while still following some of the old ways, planned to sacrifice the life of his son. But, inspiration came from Allah to say that blood sacrifice does not reach him; only piety of the heart. Furthermore, he was instructed to sacrifice a lamb and feed the people or community. This concluded many of the old ways and served as the basis of the Hajj season, belief in one G-d, and set the stage for our journey up the staircase of evolution.

Spirit of Bilal

CHAPTER 5

REGULATING MORAL LIFE

The next level of the evolutionary process of the community was called Musa in the Holy Qur'an and Moses in the Bible. With its belief in One G-d, as it was revealed to Abraham, this was the generation that made its religious journey out of thinking of the aged belief system symbolized in history as Ancient Egypt. In other words, this community left the ways of the old world and established a moral life for the community based on revelation that they received in "The Torah" which refers to the five books of Moses (Genesis, Exodus, Leviticus, Numbers and Deuteronomy).

Moral life shapes the community in the very same way the Skeleton (bones) System shapes our physical bodies. Without the Skeleton that frames our flesh and organs, we would be just a pile of flesh lying on the floor. The importance of the skeleton is to serve as an apparatus the human being needs to stand erect, and have mobility. Just as the skeleton assists the physical to move, laws help the moral life to create order in the community; without law, there is no order. It is order in the community that is the best atmosphere for progress. However, there is a danger that lies in a blind approach to this design. It brings order; however, improper use can cause the community to become rigid and philosophically resistant to new ideas.

The laws caused the community to stand tall as opposed to the people that do not adhere to laws. On the other hand, as in the case of the Hebrew speaking people, it became a priority so much so that it hardened their spirit; the community became rigid and inflexible to spiritual change. This was especially bad for that community because they had to evolve to the next level, but they could not. It proved to be a form of spiritual death. Subsequently, another stage in the growth was in order—spiritual development.

CHAPTER 6

Springing Into The Light

This community life was defined in the term Isa or Jesus; this is the generation that had the revelation called the Injil. Many believe this to be revelation, for the most part, is partially in some way contained in today's New Testament of the Bible. However, ninety percent of the New Testament is writings or reports in a form that was written by several authors such as Titus Flavius Josephus, born Josef Ben Matityahu who was a first-century Roman scholar. This was compounded by contributors and their letters such as Peter and Paul. Others information real or fictitious includes the gospel according to St. Mathews, John, Mark, Luke and several other writers or pseudonyms none of whom were Jesus. Ironically, with logic and rational thinking the hidden messages of the writings are revealed to the sober mind—the concealed or secreted concepts spring out of the darkness of confusion into the light understanding. The core of this message expressed that the laws of the previous generation were supposed to give the community shape, but, it was not the end of the growth that Allah intended for the community. "Man does not live by bread alone; the spirit of the law is more important than the letter or the law," were some the concepts of the time. They meant that moral life will guide you; however, it was not the conclusion of human spiritual growth.

It established that our nature is spiritual although we are formed out of the physical matter. The emphasis was placed on the balance between spiritual and material life. It also was the time that the concept of the soul, and its eventual return to the Creator became the focus. Also, Judgment Day alone with hell, paradise and the Shaytan (Devil) were major matters presented in this time period to this community.

As the community took form, many from the previous generation would neither accept the new thinking nor leave their old views. They remained steadfast in the religious experience, frozen in time. They named their religion Judaism and became the basis of the Jews we see today. Nevertheless, many did accept the concept of the soul and the return to Allah as the essence of the growth and new direction of the community; but, and perhaps unfortunately, they began to accept the views of the apostles or disciples of the movement: namely, Peter and Paul. It was Paul who was also called Saul in the book of Acts named this group Christians in Acts 11:26 "and when he found him, he brought him to

Antioch. So for a whole year Barnabas and Saul met with the church and taught great numbers of people. The disciples were called Christians first at Antioch".

These views became unbalanced in the sense that they were nearly all about the spiritual. There was little or no emphasis placed on the material development of the individual. The division in the community between the Jews and Christians thinkers affected the direction of the communities. In both cases, they had broken away from the linage of the original community in terms of direction.

Neither the Torah nor the Injil were complete. The two of them left the community expecting someone or something to come after them. The Torah revealed to the community that a Prophet was coming, and he would be like Moses. In the Bible, Jesus said that the Comforter would come after him. This placed the two communities in a waiting position. This was the backdrop used for the final stage; the development of a justly balanced community (Ummah).

Spirit of Bilal

CHAPTER 7

SEALING

To this point in history, the community was connected through language (Hebrew), blood relation, culture, but first and foremost through belief. They were receiving direct guidance or revelation in the form of two books: The Torah and Injil. Moreover, this is considered historical religious information; the personalities and individuals are addressed in their religious documents. "Of course neither Jewish nor Christian belief can be proved to be true simply on the basis of history," according to Ninian Smart. However, one fact remains, above all data, one of the religious personalities existed in recorded history: Prophet Muhammed Ibn Abdullah.

The final design of the Ummah would be based on the Holy Qur'an and the practical application of it by Prophet Muhammed. The Qur'an would connect all the communities from Adam to Isa. Also, it would authenticate and witness the Torah and Injil as a vital ingredient to the community. It completed the need for prophets by bringing people of different walks of life under one roof with "Peace" as its central theme. With the Qur'an as his guide, Prophet Muhammed established a justly balance community (Ummah) within 20 years.

The Ummah was founded on five principals. The first and most important is the belief in Allah as the only deity, and there is second part that says Muhammed as his Servant and Messenger. This would bring people of different ideologies together. In fact, it connected them to all the communities of the past from Adam to Isa while advancing them into the future with a powerful concept that helps shape the world. It merged theory, recorded and religious history into one. It happened in the time period that is well documented in modern time under the watchful eyes of the historians. It was the revealing of the Holy Qur'an (the last revelation) for humanity to the Last Prophet, Muhammed Ibn Abdullah.

The Qur'an addressed the issue of the past with the Jews, Christians and others. It invited them to either accept the new doctrine or follow the one that was revealed to them. It came as solution to the personal and social conditions of the society. It projected Peace as the best way of life for humanity; more progress would be made in a world of Peace than any other condition. Prophet Muhammed is an example to humanity of how to live based on the instructions and guidance in the Qur'an.

However, after the passing of Prophet Muhammed, the community life he established began to change and dissension sat in. While keeping the central idea that the Holy Qur'an is the book of Allah and Prophet Muhammed is His Messenger, many followers and supporters of the Prophet began to separate into different sects, each claiming its purity as being on the correct path in the religion. They became so opposed to one another in their thinking so much so that over the years they began to war against each other. They had lost the spirit of brotherly love that the Holy Qur'an demands, and Prophet Muhammed exemplified in his life; the oneness of humanity expressed the Holy Qur'an existed only on their lips, and not to be had in practice. It was nearly dead; it ceased to be the driving force to bring humanity together.

They became stagnant as the world moved into the twentieth century leaving them behind in their backwards thinking. However, this was not the end; it was the evidence that signaled the need for a spiritual rebirth of the original community with the spirit that defined it as a witness to Allah and the original community established by Prophet Muhammed.

Spirit of Bilal

This spirit had to be come into a new community that had not yet been born. It would be centuries and a different world before this event would take place.

CHAPTER 8

PREPARING THE HOST

Metamorphosis is a complete or marked change in appearance, character, or condition. In nature we see this process quite often. Butterflies or moths are the creatures that are most commonly associated with this process. What makes this process so remarkable is the complete change that creatures can undergo in its life. This reformation, by no means, is limited to only the physical appearance of insects or other creatures.

In the case of the butterfly, their life cycle consists of four parts with each part taken on a complete change physically. The egg is its beginning; the larva (caterpillars) is it womb stage; the pupa (cocoon) is the stage where the womb incubates inside its cocoon; the adult is the emerging out of its cocoon as a beautiful flying butterfly. In some old cultures, butterflies also symbolize rebirth into a new life after being inside a cocoon for a period of time. It is with this concept in mind that phenomenon of the physical and social metamorphosis of a people would take place to form a new community that would exemplify the spirit of the original community formed by Prophet Muhammed 1400 years ago.

The community begins as Africans on the coast of Africa and ends in America some 400 years later as a new people serving as the vessel to address humanity with this spirit.

In social development, the Africans were changed into the African-American under harsh conditions that were not of their own initiative. For some of us, our historical past resembles metamorphosis—That is to say that some of us remained in a psycho-sociological state that was formed just after racial integration; while others continued to evolve.

For example, our enslavement was the beginning; the freeing of the slave was the independent life, but not the final destination; the struggle for mental freedom was the search for cultural identity and purpose; the ultimate community that was born from that experience to address humanity was the final stage. Perhaps, this becomes clearer and better understood, when we trace the events as they unfolded in history.

We were brought from the shores of Africa over 400 years ago; dragged off in chains to a foreign land. We enter the 'Door Of No Return' a tiny Goree Island off of the city of Dakar, Senegal, and emerged on the other side of the world to a life that changed us.

When we left our homeland, we were Africans from places with our own culture that shaped our identity such as Ghana, Nigeria, and other countries and tribes from the interior and coast of Africa. Immediately, upon our arrival in the Americas, we were forced into a life of animals. Denied human rights, we were not allowed to speak our native language, carry our family names or serve the G-d of our forefathers.

The community was begun by wiping the memory of our true history from the minds of our people. Then, we were trained to behave and think of ourselves as less than human. In reality, this process was begun as an economical experiment by the Africans, Europeans and Caucasian-Americans; their motivation was money.

Cotton and tobacco were the products that would prove to be resources that would generate an enormous amount of wealth. Grown in America, they were crops that had to be picked by hand, thus requiring millions of people for the manual labor to harvest. This was the key problem that the American business community had to solve in order to create the revenue that would make America one of the riches countries in the world. They begin to import slaves from Africa by way of the slave trader.

The Slave Trader would sail from Europe; pick up slaves on the west coast of Africa. For trinkets of gold and silver, the Africans sold their people into slavery to the slave traders. After buying the slaves, they sailed to the Americas where they sold the slaves as cargo, and picked up rum, cotton and tobacco that they sold in Europe on their return trip.

The Europeans, on the other hand, needed the raw products (rum, cotton and tobacco) to manufacture goods; the rum was for consumption as alcoholic beverages; the cotton was made into clothes for men, women and children; and the tobacco was made into cigarettes, cigars, chewing and smoking tobacco. These products were sold throughout the world for a tremendous profit. This triangle between Europe, Africa and the Americas started the Industrial Age in Europe and America. However, that was not all it initiated.

Europeans, Americans and Africans had a plan, but Allah's' plan is best. Without their knowledge, a virgin community was being formed by their hands. Out of the quest for wealth, they intended to enslave a people, but actually they formed a community that Allah freed from them for His purpose. The first stage of this community began in holding pens on the west coast of Africa over four hundred years ago.

After tribal wars and small brawls between opposing tribes, the victors would sale the conquered or kidnapped to European slave traders. Then they were bounded in chains and placed in these tombs that served as holding pens. They remained confined in these coastal dungeons until the slave ships arrived to carry them to a different and new reality to become slaves in a hostile environment in North America. Their introduction to America was quite different from immigrants who came of their own free will. The impact this experience had on our ancestors affects our perception in today's America.

The enslavement of the African was a process that totally eliminated their original culture. It restricted the educational, religious, political and economical growth of our people. It was a dehumanizing experience that began on ships in chains. Packed like sardines in the bottom of wet and rat-infested ships, crammed in a space so tight, they could barely sit upright. Brought thousands of miles over the Atlantic Ocean, this terrifying voyage took between three and six months with inhuman treatment that seems beyond belief.

Imagine yourself, if you can, enclosed in a tight space for thousands of miles gasping for air. It is pitch-dark. Strangers, with their wet sweaty bodies, are pressed so tightly against you...you can hardly breathe. When you do get a breath of air, your lungs and nostrils are filled with the stench of human feces, urine and sweaty bodies that have not been bathed for weeks, even months. Imagine the smell of human vomit interrupted by the choking odor of rotten decaying bodies.

You could hear other slaves coughing, moaning and crying all through the voyage. Your thoughts of survival are broken by the rats as they run across your legs and chest. Some of your fellow travelers are bitten; perhaps even you, by these diseased infested creatures in your dark inhuman hellhole. Your hands, feet and neck are bound with chains that serve as more of a reminder of your captivity because you cannot escape anyway while the ship is tossed against the great waves of a vast ocean that rolls endlessly towards an unknown horizon.

Most Africans came to America on this type of dreadful voyage. This was the beginning of the negative attitudes formed about America and themselves by our community...this was the first assault on our psychological foundation.

After reaching the shores of America, families were separated; each member sold to different plantation owners throughout America. Stripped of the knowledge of self, America meant hundreds of years of suffering and the complete lost of our culture!

Today, we don't think much about reading a book, but the Slaves were not allowed to read, write or do anything that would benefit them or their families. Death was the punishment if they were caught doing so. This would seem to leave a negative relationship between the African-Americans and the desire to read. Contrarily, they wanted to read even more; however, the fear of death connected to the urge to learn is an enormous burden to overcome.

In his book, Our National Heritage, author Mario Pei summarized the events as he wrote, "For the Negro the only assurance was one of lifelong slavery to the cotton fields where back-breaking toil under the lash of a cruel overseer was his lot." Expressing the hopelessness, Mr. Pei continued, "The Negro knew that his children were doomed in advance to the same state of perpetual servitude that was his portion." This paints a picture of the pains and dreams of our ancestors; their outlook on life, what their thoughts were made up of, and what they had as a reward. It had a devastating effect on their minds; they could not look to the future for salvation. They were not motivated to plan for great achievements because their plans were determined by the institution of slavery. Despair and frustration are at the center of their community life. All they had were their prayers and pleads for mercy. Only Allah could rescue us from this life of slavery, suffering and death.

One thing is certain; these events had our people developing into a community that was unnatural. Survival was based on the negative and harsh aspects of environment shaping their concept of life. Seemingly doomed forever, fortunately for us, Allah's Mercy began to manifest, as the nation grew, so did the friction between the North and South. The Civil War, as the conflict was called, lasted from 1861 to 1865. The victory by the North signaled the end of slavery in America.

The bondage of slavery did not kill the spirit of Allah's Ruh that was in our people. Although their original religion was stripped from them, they turn to and adopted the religion of their slave master, Christianity. The church was a place of refuge and for community meetings. Immediately, the early builders of our community began to reform the communal life of our people.

With Allah's Mercy, our fore-parents demonstrated their ability to overcome these hardships. They awaited freedom; in theory, they were promised 40 acres and a mule. In fact, they were given a limited freedom from the burden of slavery. However, it was the taste of freedom that proved to be the ingredient that energized their growth in America.

A new life and better situations were beginning to surface. They were people of African ancestry who were stripped of their culture and nearly all memories of the homeland; they had to form a new life in America. This was the basis of the African-American community.

In the next stage of our creation, self-respect was a factor our fore-parents used for their restoration. They respected themselves as a people with a common background and goals. Unity was not an issue with them. They came together and worked for the sake of the common good or benefit of the whole.

Armed with the spirit Allah blessed them with, within twelve years after the Emancipation Proclamation in 1863, after being completely stripped of culture through dedication and hard-work, the African-American people began to educate themselves and buy a great deal of land. Author Franklin Frazier, Ph.D., on page 165 in his book entitled *The Negro In The United States*, stated that, "Between 1900 and 1910 the value of their holdings increased from $123,754,396.00 to $375,323,227.00, which was slightly higher than the relative increase in the value of white holdings." They also gained control over the trades and established a foothold in the developing steel industry in the South according to Dr. Franklin Frazier. He stated, "In southern cities the free Negroes often enjoyed a monopoly in the trades." As he continued to discuss the advances of the African-American people, Frazier pointed out that they became barbers and tailors. Additionally, they owned and operated taverns, restaurants, livery stables and catering businesses. They opened banks in New Orleans, La., Norfolk, Va. and Beaufort, SC. They had 34 banks, with deposits totaling nearly 20 million dollars.

Inventors sprang up seemingly overnight. George Washington Carver revolutionized the southern agricultural economy by introducing the products he discovered from the peanut. Because of his work, by 1938 peanuts had become a 200 million dollar industry and a chief product of Alabama. Nichol & Latimer invented an electric lamp in 1881. Elijah McCoy invented a lubricating cup that made it possible to oil machines and engines without stopping them. He received over fifty-seven patents. Jan Matzeliger invented a machine that revolutionized the manufacture of shoes throughout the world. It opened the doorway to the modern era because it made the mass production of shoes a reality. With his invention, shoe exports jumped from one million to eleven million pairs a year.

In 1897, W.B. Purvis invented the electric railway switch. Granville T. Woods invented 23 different components including a variation of a telephone transmitter and a 50,000 capacity incubator for hatching eggs.

During that period, our ancestors developed hundreds and hundreds of inventions and received many US patents. The winning attitude that they demonstrated seemed endless.

At the same time, they made remarkable advances in many other areas. Dr. E. Franklin Frazier stated: "After Emancipation, leaders emerged in churches and fraternal organizations, in education, businesses and politics." These findings of Dr. Frazier's showed that the spirit of progress was soaring though our ancestors. Furthermore, it is clear that they had self-respect and unity. The leaders in this newly formed community were concerned with the new status of their people in American society. With the unity or complete backing of their people, they took aim on the political offices or executive branches that ran the country. "The freedmen were the political leaders who were concerned with the new status of the Negro in

American society," concluded Dr. Frazier. Even after cultural destruction, our forebears exhibited endurance, strength and preeminence to bounce back and ambitiously seek the American Dream.

In the government for example, they became Senators and members of the Congress of the USA. The impact they had on southern and national government was tremendous. In the years between 1870 and 1901, there were 66 African-American members in the US Congress, State Legislature and Congress. African-Americans demonstrated in their leadership the ability and willingness to contribute their share in the building of the Nation.

In short, our people overcame the worst form of oppression in human history, and triumphed. Conditions that took hundreds of years to form during slavery were all but eliminated overnight by our ancestors. This verifies that the spirit of human survives and responds automatically even after cultural destruction; the quick rise of the African-American people demonstrates that these innate qualities will function or operate at any level of the society and freedom is the basis of its performance; the rise of our fore-parents from slavery was the birth of a new community that established itself as a productive segment of the society, and it indicated the potential impact that we could have in America.

As the stages of our creation continued, once our people began to taste success in America, they progressed so quickly that sections of the Caucasian-American communities felt threatened by this new economic and political community...this placed their monopoly of America in jeopardy. The common or everyday Caucasian-American did not feel threatened for the most part. It was the politicians who wanted to regain control of the government, and the businessmen who owned the railroad, mining, textile and many other companies. These sectors of the Caucasian-American community did not want to see the escalation of African-American progress. They envisioned our ancestor's progress as a threat of controlling a major share of the businesses and government. It was a struggle about power and money.

Because of the rivalry, the upper and middle class Caucasian-Americans began to attack our ancestors throughout the South and other parts of America. This set the stage for another major setback and a further test for the development of our community.

In their plan to regain political control in the South and maintain economical dominance over African-

Americans, some Caucasian-Americans began to devise spiteful and deadly schemes filled with bloodshed. This caused long term damage to the minds of our people for generations. Today many African-American people still view America negatively. They do not take advantage of the opportunity to go into business in this country. Even though this country was originated for business under the free-enterprise system, we are slow to join the race to establish our businesses. The effect those actions had on our situation in America is clear to this very day.

Built on the psychological impact of slavery, these schemes included the manipulation of the poor Caucasian-Americans. Their leaders influenced them to take part in a malicious form of racism against the African-American people. Dr. Frazier wrote, "The leaders who used the general unrest among the whites to attain political power succeeded in persuading the poor whites that the Negro was the cause of all their troubles." In many cases, the poor Caucasian-Americans were struggling along with African-Americans people to rebuild the South. Therefore, when their leaders began to approach them with these schemes of destruction, they rejected the schemes at first. However, after persuasive arguments, the leaders used them as pawns.

The leaders manipulated them in the strategy of their plot to gain victory.

Before the period of 1872, racism was not an institution or method of control. It became a psychological weapon directed at the low self-esteem in the poor and lower class Caucasian-Americans. They were lead into the concept of "white supremacy." They became a new destructive force that was manipulated by other of Caucasian-American leaders to suppress the spirit of the African-American People.

"White supremacy" became the rule--the white race controlling the black race and keeping its power in every way possible," according to Milton Finkelstein, Honorable Jawn A. Sandifer and Elfreda S. Wright in their book, Minorities: USA. The authors further explained, "They quickly passed laws to treat the two races in different ways." These included the Jim Crow Laws, Anti-Voting Laws, the Black Codes and the Lynch Law.

In brief, these laws controlled and suppressed the productive activities of the African-American people. "Jim Crow Laws," for example, kept the races separate. Segregated in every public place, African-Americans and Caucasian-Americans could not share in the same institutions, organizations or social activities. This ideology included railroad cars, schools, restaurants, stores, buses and any other place the Caucasian-American leaders thought would serve their purpose. They had to drink from separate fountains. They set up separate public schools. This allowed the Caucasian to take nearly all the money supplied by the State Education System and funnel these resources to now all white schools. In contrast, they gave the African-American schools a small fraction of the amount they received, which created a poorer and inferior educational system in the African-American community.

"Anti-Voting Laws" eliminated African-American people from voting. This gave the political power to Caucasian-American people on a silver platter. First, they introduced a tactic that imposed a poll tax and other taxes. Established quickly, these taxes had to be paid one month before the election. Second, a literacy test was set-up. To qualify for voting, a citizen had to read and interpret the state and federal constitutions. The elected officials who determined whether a voter interpreted these provisions properly were Caucasian-American.

The "grandfather clause" included in most state constitutions excused some voters from this process. This clause stated that if a person or his grandfather served in the armies, United States or the Confederacy, he could vote. Of course, this excluded our ancestors from voting because they were ex-slaves and their grandfathers were slaves. They did not serve in either army.

The forerunner to most laws designed to retard African-American progress was the "Black Codes." These laws brought back the kind of lifestyle that was prevalent under slavery. For example, the police could arrest and take back any African-Americans who quit their job to their employer. African-Americans paid a fine of $50 if they did not have a job. If they could not pay this fine, someone else could pay it. However, who ever paid the fine, the ex-slave worked for them under this law. Usually, a Caucasian-American paid it.

A $1 tax was levied on everyone. If any African-American could not pay it, the same principle applied as other fines. Result, the ex-slave worked for the Caucasian-American who paid it. Male children under 18 had to work for the former master until age 21 and female until they were 18.

Under this Black Code, there were no inter-racial marriages. All the old slave codes remained in effect. Treated as if they were still slaves and punished accordingly, African-Americans continued to the struggled for freedom.

Coupled to these codes was the inhumane "Lynch Law." Under this law, African-Americans were dragged by the thousands before the courts and sentenced to death without trials. Mobs were given keys to jails to torture, hang, shoot or mutilate the accused in the most horrifying ways.

Organizations such as the Ku Klux Klan (KKK) were born out of this mentality and their method was terror. This was one of the world's first and worst terrorist groups.

The KKK was a group of Caucasian-American people organized in 1865 in Pulaski, Tennessee. They burned, murdered and whipped the African-American people in an attempt to halt their economic and political growth.

Continuing their argument, authors Finkelstein, Sandifer and Wright pointed out, "Within twenty years Southern states had passed laws to keep black farm workers on the land, to keep their wages low and to punish them for any word or action against a white person." They stated, while discussing the position that the Supreme Court took on this issue, "In 1883 the Court ruled that the federal government could not pass and enforce civil rights laws." In essence, the effect of these actions lasted until the 1960's. They gave the southern states a free hand in the treatment of African-American people.

These rules opened doors to an era of injustice, violence, death and the worst example of a democratic society in history. Woven into American life, the fabric of segregation and discrimination robbed the African-American people of their place in the procession of human progress. For generations, it deprived them of their human rights; freedom, justice and equality. This treatment was another attempt to permanently suppress and destroy economic competition.

In this stage of our creation, even under these conniving and cruel conditions, the strength and spirit of the African-American's character began to radiate. Building on some advances made during reconstruction, our ancestors developed an economical foundation. Relentlessly, they began to flourish and rise above the horrendous scheme of racism. As a step toward independence, they managed their schools, businesses, hospitals and trades.

In education, for example, they established thousands of elementary schools throughout the South. Also, in most major cities, they had as many as three or more high schools composed of an all African-American staff, from the school principals to the custodians.

Contributing to this tremendous effort, with their professional and educational backgrounds were courageous people like George Washington Carver, Mary McLeod Bethune, Booker T. Washington, W.E.B. Du Bois and Frederick Douglas. With less Federal funds then the Caucasian-American community, they and others helped to erect colleges and universities for African-American people. From this activity we now have over 107 traditional African-American colleges and universities in the USA; Howard University, Fisk University, Southern University, Tuskegee, Atlanta University, Clark University, Morehouse College, Spellman College and Morris Brown University located in Atlanta, Georgia are just a few of them. This accomplishment in education was one never matched by any other people in history under such adverse conditions.

As in education, the African-American people made similar progress in business under segregation. This is another accomplishment our ancestors achieved that we, their descendants, can hold with pride. As slaves, they could not participate in the business of economic development. Once they were free of oppression, their business interest grew tremendously.

In the early years of their freedom, they gained some business experience. Also, they received some support from other African-Americans who lived in the Free states and some Caucasian-Americans.

Under the restrictions of segregation and with hard work, our community built an economic foundation that was a greater threat to certain Caucasian-American groups than ever before. This progress carried the seeds of separate economies. The possibility of an independent African-American economy was beginning to emerge. This generated the memories of feared secession of the South from the Union in the mind of some Caucasian-Americans.

This was apparent, when in the 1900s; an all African-American community in Tulsa, Oklahoma built a financial district. By 1913, they produced some of the richest families in America. Known as "Negro Wall Street," they acquired a great deal of land, independently owned and operated their businesses, banks and schools.

Then in 1921, their entire town was burned down by the Caucasian-Americans, people were murdered, businesses destroyed, their community lay waste in the ashes of hatred. This heinous act carries the distinction of being the first American city to be bombed from within its boundaries. The town then established rules and laws that would never allow the African-American people to rebuild, as reported by "Tony Brown's Journal" dated 3rd Quarter 1985 on page 12. As devastating as this heartless action was to the African-American community, it did not halt their rise.

In 1924, an African-American organization, the National Negro Business League, met to celebrate its Silver Jubilee in Chicago. African-Americans operated 65,000 businesses and had accumulated wealth amounting to $1,700,000,000. These facts are in Dr. Frazier's book, quoted in the "Literary Digest," Volume 81 (1924) on page 62 in the article, "growth of Negro Business."

Between the years of 1888 and 1934, African-Americans owned and operated 134 banks. With assets of 13 million dollars in 14 southern states, they had banks in the District of Columbia. This formed a valuable foundation for the potential economic growth of the community.

Following the progress of the banks was the insurance companies.   North Carolina Mutual, Mississippi Life, Standard Life, Bankers Fire, National Benefit Life, Liberty Life, Supreme Life and Northeastern Life are some of the insurance companies that accumulated millions of dollars and hired thousands of African-American employees. Following the insurance companies, there were hundreds of retail establishments, small manufacturing companies and the trades.

Despite the gloom with which our ancestors viewed the political world after being forced out of government by the new Anti-Voting laws, they relentlessly set up successful businesses and educational facilities in the country. It had the potential to exceed the economic wealth of most of today's Third World Countries. Our fore-parents achieved this by establishing organizations within the community. The formation of fraternal groups, hundreds (in some cases, thousands) of religious groups, sports teams (Athletic Associations), intellectual groups, scientific associations and business enterprises were the beginnings of an independent community in America.

Their personal ambitions helped many them become millionaires. Atlanta, Georgia and other major cities throughout America was the oasis for the African-American professionals. They established business organizations as models of progress for African-American people.

In addition, they had to build a lifestyle with less financial support than any other ethnic group. They accomplished this task without equal economical, political and educational opportunities. Nevertheless, under segregation, their spirit rose to face the challenge, and this stage our community was well on the way.

CHAPTER 9

EATING FORBIDDEN FRUIT

The community had to develop a suitable mental state to be able to cope with and change the world in which it would find itself. The world had succumbed to one of the most destructive forces in human society, Racism. Philosophically and practically, the majority of the world was dominated by racial supremacy either covertly or overtly. The concept of racial superiority has corrupted human values, especially those that address human equality. It hinders the people of the world in their effort to strive for human excellence.

The concept, The Original Man is the Asiatic Black Man, the G-d and owner of the earth, was a good method to develop a positive self-image in the culturally depleted African-American people; but, in the supreme race concept, it carried with it the seed of racism which will inevitably lead to the destruction of human values and progress in the community.

Imam Mohammed knew that he had to rid the community of the deadly force of racism for their survival. He directed the community's attention to the damage of racism and the psychology behind it. He achieved this task over several years with a keen sense of awareness of their present state of mind and a barrage of anti-racist concepts desired to free the mind. This began with understanding racism and its nature.

Racism, which begins simply as racial pride, is the Achilles heel of a wholesome human society. Initially, as racial or ethnic pride that develops a positive attitude in the group, in the long run, it changes because it carries with it the germ of prejudice or animosity against people who belong to other groups or races. Additionally, it serves as a tool that breaks down the moral and ethical values, and prevents humanity from bonding as one family.

It fosters the idea that one is superior by virtue of one's birth; moreover, and even more harmful, the idea is then connected to the "Divine," the belief that it is the will of the Creator. There are many historical events and ideologies that led to this concept. Blood ties are one of the many.

Blood ties are not new in the thinking of the general public. One of the earliest and perhaps most used is the idea that **"Blood is thicker than water."** Although commonly used by the western world, it comes from an old German proverb, *"Blut ist dicker als Wasser."* Generally, it means that the bonds of family and common ancestry are stronger than those bonds between unrelated people. In essence, water represents emotional bonds, and Blood is the biological or physical bond to ancestry.

In 1859, Navy Commodore Josiah Tattnall use the proverb in his defense of his action to give aid of his American ship to a British ship during an attack on the Chinese although this was thereby infringing strict American neutrality.

"Blood is thicker than water" is a recognizable proverb that has surpassed the test of time. The generally accepted interpretation of blood is even stronger than the bond of marriage. Various interpretations include Lydgate's: "Relationships within the family are stronger than any other kind." The idea of blood includes bloodlines, bad blood and even blood brother (either two males related by birth, or two or more men not related by birth, but who swear loyalty to one another). This line of thinking is one of foundations on which racism anchored itself. However, it is certainly not the only tool to feed racial supremacy.

Racism carries a very intoxicating emotion that causes pride and encourages the concept of invincibility just as the Chinese philosophy of yang that is the principle of light, heat, motivation, and masculinity. However, according to that philosophy, existing along with the yang is yin, the counterpart of that is the principle. Yin is of darkness, negativity, and femininity. This same dual nature exists in racism.

Eventually, the racist sees themselves as supreme and ruler of the other groups or even mankind. This attitude breeds the desire to control and rule the others through language, psychology or brute force. This continues, as in the case of Nazi Germany, until the world of humanity rises up and crushes it with force. However, truth has the same power to illuminate racism from the hearts and minds of the masses by exposing it to the light of truth and understanding; to do that, it is most important to understand the nature of racism and how to identify it.

Another form of racism that forestalls solidarity in the world can be seen in Darwinism and survival of the fittest concept. This was an idea that arose from the theory of Charles Darwin an English naturalist who lived in England in the 1800's. Darwin established that all species of life have descended over time from common ancestry. His scientific theory suggested that a branching pattern of evolution occurred from a process that he called natural selection. This idea was captured in his book "*On the Origin of Species*" published 1859.

This is the shorten version of the title as it is more commonly known. The actually title is "***On the Origin of Species by Means of Natural Selection, or the Preservation of Favoured Races in the Struggle for Life.***"

As you can see, the title indicates that this is another strong basis for the fever of racism to emerge. A summary of Darwin's theory can be found in the Wikipedia online encyclopedia as it states, "Individuals less suited to the environment are less likely to survive and less likely to reproduce; individuals more suited to the environment are more likely to survive and more likely to reproduce and leave their inheritable traits to future generations, which produces the process of natural selection (inference)."

While Darwin claimed he did not approve of slavery or the mistreatment of native people, in the 1930s and 1940s, his works was the corner stone of modern evolutionary theory, and the source for the racist mind to gather fuel to build its infernal.

Wikipedia again reports, "Critics derided his description of a struggle for existence as a Malthusian justification for the English industrial capitalism of the time." The link became even stronger as the term *Darwinism* was used for the evolutionary ideas of others such as

"Survival of the Fittest" as free-market progress is from Herbert Spencer, a contemporary of Darwin. Also common for that time, were strong racist ideas of human development by Ernst Haeckel.

The views of Spencer and Haeckel were mild as compared to those of Antoinette Brown Blackwell. Blackwell considered the European civilization as one of great value, and colonization as spreading its benefits. He also saw the extermination of what he called savage people who did not become civilized as a necessity. According to David Frawley, as he reflected of the time in these words, "The Nineteenth Century was the Era of European Imperialism. Many Europeans did in fact believe that they belonged to a superior race and that their religion, Christianity, was a superior religion and all other religions were barbaric."

"The Europeans," Frawley continued, "felt that it was their duty to convert non-Christians, sometimes even if it required intimidation, force or bribery."

The points the Frawley made were very revealing as to the mindset of the European who became the mentor for the world it conquered and colonized. Their relationship with non-European was governed by their racist view of the world. Frawley addressed it in these words, "European thinkers of the era were dominated by a racial theory of man, which was interpreted primarily in terms of color. They saw themselves as belonging to a superior 'white' or Caucasian race."

Darwin's theories presented this as natural, and were used to support the concepts, opinions and ideologies such as laissez-faire, dog-eat dog capitalism, racism, warfare, colonialism and imperialism. While this may not have been Darwin's intent, nevertheless, it was another foundation on which racism reared its ugly head.

The ugly and destructive force of racism occurred in nearly every society and country. It is not the exclusive trait of one group or another. It evolved out of our human nature. It grew out of our natural power to discriminate from primitive times. As early man evolved, we began to use our rational mind to figure out the creation. The power to discriminate is part of the rational power; in fact, it is a key component to our ability to discern what is beneficial. It is the treatment or consideration of, or making a distinction in favor of or against.

This ability to see fine distinctions and differences is responsible for our survival and progress. Without it we are lost. All animals have this power. In psychology, it is viewed as the ability to perceive and respond to differences among stimuli. It is considered a more advanced form of learning than generalization.

Discrimination is the tool we use to make choices about our lives. We have the power of choice and the ability to fulfill it. From primitive time until the present, this has been our gift from Allah. We must use it wisely. To do that, it is important the human being exercise our Moral Conscience and human ethics in order to keep our human composure. Unfortunately, far to many people and civilizations chose not to be led by their morals. As a result, it was the form of discrimination that is founded on prejudicial treatment of an individual based solely on their membership in a certain group or category; thus, ushering in racism.

Racism has existed throughout human history and in nearly every society or social group. It has influenced wars, slavery, the formation of nations, and legal codes.

However, it was the western culture that carried its harmful effects both psychological and physical as they colonized the world.

On this point, historians agree that during the past 500-1000 years, racism on the part of Western powers toward non-Westerners has had a far more significant impact on history than any other form of racism. The most notorious example of racism by the West has been slavery, particularly the enslavement of Africans in the New World (slavery itself dates back thousands of years). This enslavement was accomplished because of the racist belief that Black Africans were less fully human than white Europeans and their descendants. More distressing is the fact that this belief is rooted in imagines of divine and their connection to the Caucasian race.

Divinity runs constant through human consciousness regardless of location, isolation or era in time. It is as if the belief in divinity that motivates societies to create cultural tenets, laws, rituals, science, math, calendars, and agricultural advances amongst other things. It provides a society with a sense of cohesiveness and purpose. However, whenever, a divinity identifies a race connected to that divinity, where as other races are not, it becomes the deepest and most severely damaging form of racism.

Some religions such as Al-Islam has forbidden the use of making images of any form of divine especially Allah. However, others such as Christianity still use images to represent divine (relating to the worship or service of G-d). This is referred to as the practice of worshiping a deity through images.

Darwinism was a minor problem for the African-American when compared to the impact that this form of worship does. The idea of white supremacy based on a natural order of selective breeding, most take a backseat to the idea of white supremacy defined in a white images of divine (G-d, Angels, Prophets and Saints) that was engraved in the sub-conscience mind of the African-American that cause their conscience to respond in favor of the white racist. No matter the situation, the African-American would in a confused state as long as they look at the racist in the same image as that of the divine.

Marcus Garvey noted that it is natural for a culture to propagate divinity in its own image. It is unnatural, however, to force others to see divinity in the same way, a way that does not reflect them.

No longer were they in the physical changes of slavery, but the damage done to the African in America by the painful social and psychological transformation would to be extremely difficult to reverse even after they were free. Even as social groups attempted to break its grip, racism affected their decision or formation in terms of ideology.

African-Americans have struggled for hundreds of years to get from under white supremacy and their racial discrimination against non-Caucasians. However, in their struggle, African-Americans experienced some of the same attitudes toward Caucasians-Americans as those manifested by the Caucasian American. The one that most noticeable was the reverse of "white supremacy" into "black supremacy."

This was a major shift in the African-American, America and other social groups especially in the large urban cities. This shift took place in the most exciting and fascinating time the history of the African-American community; it flipped the psychic of America upside down; it began the rescue the mind of the African-American Community from white supremacy.

This occurred over a period of forty-nine years, between 1910 and 1959; it was when the Black supremacy movements had gained such momentum in that short time period it got attention of the national news media and the world.

Ultimately, facing the rising tide of racism and a quarter of a million African-Americans turning to black supremacy as an alternative, in 1959, Mike Wallace and Louis Lomax were television journalists for *News Beat*, a program on WNTA-TV in New York, produced a program called "The Hate That Hate Produced."

Some years later, Mike Wallace (a Caucasian American) became well known as a CBS journalist, and for co-hosting TV news magazine program on CBS called "60 Minutes." His co-host was Harry Reasoner.

Meanwhile, previous to "60 Minutes," it was Lomax (an African American) who told Wallace about the Nation of Islam, and Wallace became interested in the group. Lomax was given rare access to the organization.

"The Hate That Hate Produced" aired in five parts during the week of July 13–17, 1959, and was repeated several days later.

Wallace was the lead reporter and narrator of the program. Lomax filmed the events and interviewed the principals, namely, The Honorable Elijah Muhammad leader of the Nation of Islam, and James R. Lawson president of the Unit African Nationalist Movement. He also interviewed Malcolm X, the National representative of Elijah Muhammed.

No immediate solutions drawn, it was obvious to the listeners and viewers that the problem and the African-American's answer to it did not spring up over night.

CHAPTER 10

CHANGING THE GAME

The response to racism in America against the African-American was launched first by individuals who establish powerful groups and organizations. While there were several, two of those great pioneers were Booker T. Washington and William Edward Burghardt Du Bois.

Booker Taliaferro Washington, one of the must courageous and steadfast African-Americans, was born into slavery April 5, 1856 and passed at the age of 59 on November 14, 1915. The African-American community will be forever indebted to this American educator, author, orator, and political leader. His autobiography, *"Up From Slavery,"* first published in 1901, is still widely read today.

Washington was a dominant figure of the African-American community in the United States from 1890 to 1915, especially as an individual who had a great concern for the progress of his people as well as himself. He viewed the advancement of the African-American as a matter of becoming more educated and furthers the development of their skills as the path to a brighter future in America. He worked closely with wealthy Caucasians who were willing to help finance those concerns and objectives. He raised educational funds from this group as he built a nationwide network of supporters in many black communities, with black ministers, educators and businessmen composing his core supporters.

The funds raised were use to establish and operate thousands of small community schools and institutions of higher education for the betterment of African-American people throughout the South such as Tuskegee University.

Washington believed deeply in the concept of self help; this was the path that would lead the African-American community from poverty to success. He exemplified his idea when at the age of 25 he was selected to be the leader of the new all-black Tuskegee Normal and Industrial Institute by its organizers. He purchased a former plantation which became the permanent site of the campus.

He directed his students literally built their own school: constructing classrooms, barns and outbuildings; and growing their own crops and raising livestock; both for learning and to provide for most of the basic necessities. This practice fit perfectly into his core belief that the African-Americans should concentrate all their energies on industrial education, and accumulation of wealth, and the conciliation of the South.

While he believed that cooperation with supportive Caucasian-American was the only way to overcome pervasive racism in the long run, in the same period, others, such as W. E. B. Du Bois expressed that Washington was too accommodating to the interest of Caucasian people. This Issue did not always stand between them. At one time, he partly, along with Du Bois, organized the "Negro Exhibition" at the 1900 "Exposition Universelle" in Paris. They entered a photography display of pictures taken by photographer Frances Benjamin Johnston that depicted the African-Americans' contribution to the American society. However, from that point, Du Bois took assertive turn on the road to progress; he believed the African-Americans should take the same classical liberal arts education as Caucasians, along with voting rights and civic equality.

Du Bois was born February 23, 1868. He was an intellectual leader of the African-American community in America. He believed and professed that the progress of the African-American people will depend on the degree in which we encouraged and taught our children to think. In multiple roles as civil rights activist, Pan-Africanist, sociologist, historian, author, and editor, Du Bois was deeply concerned by the social condition in America.

Biographer David Levering Lewis wrote, "In the course of his long, turbulent career, W. E. B. Du Bois attempted virtually every possible solution to the problem of twentieth-century racism—scholarship, propaganda, integration, national self-determination, human rights, cultural and economic separatism, politics, international communism, expatriation, third world solidarity."

Du Bois graduated from Harvard, where he earned his Ph.D in History, making him Harvard's first African-American to earn a Ph.D. Later he became a professor of history and economics at Atlanta University. He became the head of the National Association for the Advancement of Colored People (NAACP) in 1910. This was one of the first of several organizations that the African-American community developed to free their mind and body; it still has an important presence for social change today in 2011. It has fought and won many legal battles for the community.

DuBois was the founder and editor of the NAACP's journal *The Crisis*. *Du Bois* campaigned to increase political representation for Africa-Americans in order to guarantee civil rights, and the formation of Africa-American elite that would work for the progress of the African -American people.

"In 1934, Du Bois left the magazine to return to teaching at Atlanta University, after writing two essays published in the *Crisis* suggesting that black separatism could be a useful economic strategy," according to Wikipedia.

Du Bois and Mary White Ovington were co-founders of (NAACP). To the dismay of some, Ovington was Caucasian-American.

However, she was a social reformer, supporter of women rights and involved in the anti-slave movement. Ovington became involved in the campaign for civil rights in 1890 after hearing Frederick Douglass speak in a Brooklyn church.

A powerful speaker, Frederick Douglass was another African-American who led the fight against racism. Although, he was 50 years Du Bois senior, he was a leader of the abolitionist movement, gaining recognition for his dazzling oratory and incisive antislavery writing. He was one of the fortunate Africans to escape from slavery. As Douglass passed the torch of freedom to the next generation, so in time it became Du Bois' turn to give over the quest for the liberation of the African-

American community to incoming bearers of truth such as Timothy Drew, better known as Noble Drew Ali.

Parallel to DuBois and the NAACP movement there were some African-Americans that sort to solve social issues of their community through the religion and confront the divinity concept head-on as a viable course of action. The religion that some of them chose was Al-Islam.

Al-Islam was not new to America; many of the slaves brought to colonial America from Africa were Muslims. By 1800, some 500,000 Africans arrived in what became the United States. Historians estimate that between 15 to 30 percent of all enslaved African men, and less than 15 percent of the enslaved African women, were Muslims. These enslaved Muslims stood out from their compatriots because of their "resistance, determination and education." It is also recorded that some Muslims freed from slavery fought in the "Civil War."

From the 1880s to 1914, several thousand Muslims came to the United States from the Ottoman Empire, and from parts of South Asia; they did not form distinctive settlements, and most assimilated into the wider American society.

Neither the Muslims that were enslaved on the plantations nor those who immigrated to America were able to solve the overwhelming issue facing the African-American community.

In the case of the enslaved Muslims, the records show that most of them were converted to Christianity in either the first or second generation. As to the Immigrant Muslims, they kept a low profile and fused into the general society. They did not want to start what may be viewed as trouble. However, in either case, the two groups would have been playing with the deck stacked against them as in the case with Du Bois, Douglas and nearly all of those that came before them. While they knew it was a race issue, they just did not know how deep.

This left the African-American with one preferable alternative, establish and develop Al-Islam as an indigenous American. The first of these to do so was Noble Drew Ali.

Noble Dew Ali was born January 8, 1886 in North Carolina as Timothy Drew. Historians have different versions of his birth; one account claims his ancestry as being the son of two former slaves; another describes him as being the son of a Moroccan Muslim father and a Cherokee mother.

Three years after DuBois founded the NAACP, Timothy Drew, at the age of 27, calling himself the Prophet Noble Drew Ali founded the Moorish Science Temple of America in 1913 in Newark, New Jersey. Drew Ali said to his members, "To you, I am an Angel of Allah sent to bring you the everlasting Gospel of Allah." He continued that thought, "Indeed, the Angel was born amongst the very nation He was sent to redeem." This was the beginning of a long awaited rescue call that many in the African-American community yearned for.

Drew Ali, a studious strategist, created his religion that he said was a sect of Al-Islam, although, he used elements from other disciplines such as Buddhism, Christianity, Freemasonry, Gnosticism and Taoism. By combining certain elements of major religious traditions, he developed a message of personal transformation, racial pride and uplift for the African-Americans.

The primary tool he used to attract the African-American was the belief that they were descended from the Moors (rather than sub-Saharan Africans) and thus was originally Islamic. Along with this, he gave them a new identity in order to begin to build a positive self-image. For example, he added the name Bey or El to the surnames. This was one method of disconnecting them from negative identity of slavery, segregation and white supremacy.

To attract the African-American community to accept his form of Al-Islam, he compiled "**The *Circle Seven Koran*"** which is the holy scripture of the Moorish Science Temple of America. Its cover featured a red "7" surrounded by a blue circle. With great care, he compiled his book so that it was not confused with The "Holy Qur'an" revealed to the Prophet Muhammed 1400 years ago.

In the spelling of his book, he used the English "K" rather the than Arabic letter "Qaf" which would sound like the "Q" in Queen or Québec. Furthermore, he used the "o" in his Koran. There is no "O" in the Arabic language. Therefore, after close observation, it is clear that he was not trying to rewrite the original Qur'an, and he did not want to infringe upon the integrity of the Muslim Holy Book.

Drew Ali was a noted Egyptian Adept (highly proficient or expert at Egyptology), and traveled East around the age of 16. At this time he was initiated, and later became an Adept. The first nineteen chapters of the Circle Seven were compiled from what is known as the Aquarian Gospel of Jesus the Christ was transliterated, and published in 1908 by esoteric Ohio preacher Levi

Dowling. Chapters 20–44 were compiled from the Economy of Life, or the text known as *"Unto Thee I Grant."*

Noble Drew Ali compiled these ancient texts into a pamphlet, allowing them to be lessons for the so-called blacks of America.

He drew thousands to this brand of religion tailored especially for them. It enriched them psychologically as it connected them to the divine. Those who adhered to the religion were called Moors. This was perhaps the first elements to reverse white divinity in the mind of a segment of the African-American community.

Drew Ali taught his followers to "face east when praying, regard Friday as their holy day, and call their god Allah. The Moorish-Americans were not obligated to follow Al-Islam completely. They pray five times a day, and travel to Mecca only if they choose to do so. He allowed some hymns sung adapted from traditional Christian hymns common in black churches.

He moved to Chicago, establishing a center there, where it expanded rapidly. The **Moorish Science Temple of America** membership was estimated at 35,000, in Philadelphia, Detroit, Newark, Washington, DC and Chicago, with one third of them in Chicago. The expansion of the Moorish Science Temple arose from the search for identity as hundreds of thousands of African-Americans from the rural South sought to establish themselves in urban regions of the United States

According to Drew Ali, Jesus and his followers were Asiatic. "Asiatic" was the term Drew used for all dark or olive-colored people; he labeled all whites as European. Carrying his concept to unite his people, he taught them to become better citizens and reject derogatory labels, such as "Black", "colored", and "Negro".

 He urged Americans of all races to reject hate and embrace love. He believed that Chicago would become a second Mecca.

Drew, in 16 years, built his organization. He proclaimed that, "Until my Moors are free in their own home the worst is yet to come. The United States owe the Moors a great debt; they must pay in compound interest. The United States has one more war to win". The next year Drew Ali passed.

Although he passed in 1929 at age 43, the organization was strong. However, by the late 20th century, it had stop attracting the young people. Yet, according to some of their members, there are 800 members in the four major cities; and approximately one million members nationwide in 260 temples.

Before his death, Drew Ali had made several progressive achievements for the African-American people. For example, at the 1928 Pan American Conference For Indigenous Nations, he registered The Moorish Americans, as a New Nation and Sovereign power. This was the first time that a segment of the African-American community declared itself a separate nation.

They claimed their one free National Name of "Moorish Americans." This marks the first time the ex-slaves' proper status has been truly represented since the abolishment of U. S. Slavery. This event is a reflection of one of the many achievements of Drew Ali.

Noble Drew Ali declared, "This is a new era of time now and all men now must proclaim their free national name to be recognized by the government and the nations of the earth." With this international proclamation of Independence, Drew Ali paved the way for the Moorish Americans, and thousand of African-Americans to come...they must finish freeing themselves in order to assure true freedom.

He developed an organization that inspired those that followed him. His Supreme Grand Governor was Lomax

Bey, who later became known as Professor Muhammad Ezaldeen, one of the most notable.

Lomax Bey was a Moorish American over a Moorish Science Temple of American under leadership of Noble Drew Ali. After the passing of Drew Ali, Lomax Bey continued to study and develop the principals. While focusing on ethnic or racial identity, he differed in one major way; he chose to follow the The Holy Qur'an as revealed to Prophet Muhammed of 1400 years ago.

He studied in Egypt at Al-Ahzar University where he received his professorship. He changed his name to Professor Muhammad Ezaldeen.

Ezaldeen is the Founder Addeynu Allahe-Universal Arabic Assoc., Inc. He was also an Egyptologist, Educator, and Community Activist. He founded the A.A.-U.A.A., Inc. on August 18, 1938 in Newark, New Jersey. Later, he moved to southern New Jersey and there reestablished the national headquarters for the A.A.-U.A.A., Inc. He taught Al-Islamic religion, Arabic, and Eastern heritage and culture.

It is reported that he could recite the Holy Qur'an from cover to cover. While at Al-Ahzar he learned to read, rather than just interpret, the writings within the walls of the ancient pyramids. Thus he was able to learn the history of mankind as perceived by the ancient Egyptian culture.

When he completed his study, he returned to the United States with this knowledge. With the new concept, he began to trace the history and heritage of the African-American people. Rather than Moorish decent, he claimed that the true heritage of the African-American was Hamitic-Arab people; consequently, he would deliver religious teachings, and it would restore them to their divine heritage and identity.

The A.A.-U.A.A., Inc. has spawned many Al-Islamic groups and organizations that are spreading his messages of identity, heritage, and self-awareness.

"The aims and objectives of A.A.-U.A.A., Inc. shall be to teach Eastern Culture; to build and maintain a National institution; to educate and rescue every Hamitic-Arab and bring him back to the highest type of civilization, where he once was; to promote love and good will among the Hamitic-Arabs at home and abroad and thereby to maintain the integrity and sovereignty of Arabia; to disseminate the ancient Arabic and Eastern culture among its members; to correct abuses, relieve oppression and carve for ourselves and our posterity a destiny comparable with our idea of perfect manhood and Allah's purpose in creating us, that we may now save ourselves from the curse of our creator," according to the Aims and purpose published by The A.A.-U.A.A., Inc.

They contend, "We, the Arab-Americans, in order to effect Unity, Solidarity, Liberty, Freedom, and to secure Justice and to maintain the Integrity of Arabia, which is our divine heritage, do hereby establish and ordain this Constitution for Addeynu Allahe - Universal Arabic Association, Incorporated."

Professor Ezaldeen claimed that the Hamitic people are descended from the Prophet Ham; the third son of the Prophet Noah—this is the origin of the Hamitic-Arab. These are the descendants from a royal daughter of Pharaoh of the lineage of Misrine named Hajar and the wife of Prophet Abraham. Professor Ezaldeen passed in 1957.

He was one of many said to have been inspired by Drew Ali. The influence of Drew Ali stretches into other organizations that developed during and after his time such as the founding of the Nation of Islam, Fard Muhammad. Fard created competition for members. However, the one that came before Fard was a powerful and very intelligent Jamaican by the name of Marcus Garvey.

Garvey was born in Jamaica in 1887, and came to the United States by way of England in 1916. He was a publisher, journalist, entrepreneur, Black Nationalist, Pan-Africanist, and orator. Although Garvey's movement lost its luster after his passing, his of separatism caught on to a few organization of the future, especially the teachings of The Honorable Elijah Muhammad in the Nation of Islam.

Garvey believed in separatism of the people of African ancestry. His movement focused on those of African ancestry to "redeem" Africa for Africans. Along with inspiring a global mass movement and economic empowerment, Garvey was unique in advancing a Pan-African philosophy.

He was founder of the Universal Negro Improvement Association and African Communities League (UNIA-ACL). This movement that took place in the 1920s; it was the largest movement of people of African descent, even larger than the Civil Rights Movement. The Garvey Movement was a spring board for splinter groups such as The African Nationalist Pioneer Movement headed by Carlos Cooks, The Garvey Club, United Sons and Daughters of Africa, and the First Africa Corps.

During a trip to Jamaica, in 1965, Martin Luther King Jr., one of the world greatest social activist and champion for the African-American struggle for human dignity, visited the shrine of Marcus Garvey. In a speech he told the audience that Garvey "was the first man of color to lead and develop a mass movement. He was the first man on a mass scale and level to give millions of Negroes a sense of dignity and destiny. And make the Negro feel he was somebody."

Garvey's memory has been kept alive. The events of his impact are in schools, colleges, highways, and buildings in Africa, Europe, the Caribbean, and the United States that have been named in his honor. His UNIA red, black, and green flag has been adopted as the Black Liberation Flag.

Garvey's movement brought excitement and the hope a solution to the African-American problems in America. It answered some the questions that the Christian religion organizations could not. Garvey who was raised Methodist and later became Catholic found the churches were not the answer. Although, African-Americans churches were formed and separated from Caucasian churches because of discrimination, the religions could not solve the problems of racism or free their minds from the concept of white supremacy.

Garvey was deported back to Jamaica after having several charges one of which was mail fraud. The charges were a tactic used to rid the country of what they consider a problem. After two strokes, Garvey died on June 10, 1940. Perhaps, he will be most gratefully and best remembered in the words of John Henrik Clarke as he wrote, "We must regain our confidence in ourselves as a people and learn again the methods and arts of controlling nations. We must hear again Marcus Garvey calling out to us: UP! UP! YOU MIGHTY RACE! YOU CAN ACCOMPLISH WHAT YOU WILL!"

During the time of Garvey, Drew Ali, DuBois, Booker T. Washington, another piece of the puzzle fell into place, the idea of a Black Man as G-d. This idea was brought to it fullness by a Christian Preacher called Father Divine.

Little is known about **Father Divine's** early life; even his date of birth and real name which maybe George Baker according to some researchers is somewhat unclear. He was believed to have been born in Georgia sometime in 1876. Other than the consensus that he passed in September 1965, what is known about him begins with his assertion that he was "The Messenger" of G-d, and ended as he declared that he himself was the only true expression of G-d's spirit. In essence, he declared himself a g-d; he was the first African-American to state that he was G-d in the flesh.

He got this idea from the Bible in 1 John 4:15 to mean G-d was in everyone. The verse states, "Whoever shall confess that Jesus is the Son of God, God dwells in him and he in God."

Father Divine started preaching in 1913. Later, he established his "Peace Movement; It then became known as the "International Peace Mission Movement."

Divine moved to Harlem, New York where he had accumulated significant following in the black community. Purchasing several hotels, which they called "Heavens", members could live and seek jobs inexpensively. The movement also opened several budget enterprises including restaurants and clothing shops that sold cheaply as compared to the market prices. These proved very successful in the depression. Economical, cash-only businesses were actually part of Father Divine's doctrine. He and his disciples formed a commune in a black middle-class apartment building. He forbade sex, alcohol, tobacco, and gambling among those who were living with him.

By 1934 branches had opened in Los Angeles, California, and Seattle, Washington, and gatherings occurred in France, Switzerland, Canada, and Australia. Some estimates claimed he had nearly 2 million followers; while others sited tens of thousands. Nonetheless,

Father Divine had a massive movement that raised a great deal of money and eventually political clout.

The time had come. While all of these men exemplified the one man rule concept, it was Devine with the Black Man as G-d and strict moral life style; Garvey with his separatist policy and nationhood; and Drew Ali with the lost African-Americans from their Moorish ancestry and Asiatic roots and the establishment hierarchy as the central structure of the organization. The vehicle of hope was now filled with necessary components to obliterate the "white supremacy" concept once and for all.

CHAPTER 11

FORMATTING The PLAN

We were Christians by default because it was not our original religion; at the time, it was our only choice. However, it served a purpose for a time; it was shaped to fit one part of a far greater plan. It had become necessary to use old traditions and adapt them to a new purpose.

As the Qur'an says, "We breathed into her of Our Spirit and We made her and her son a Sign for all peoples." We know that the African-American community fits this symbolic type, Mary. The next step is the son, Jesus or a community to proclaim Allah's word. This is echoed by the Bible in these words, "Behold, a virgin shall be with child, and shall bring forth a son, and they shall call his name Emmanuel, which being interpreted is god with us." In this case, as Imam Mohammed mentioned, "the son is a follower of G-d as a son follows his father." For this reason, a son (another community having the "Word" from Allah in it) had to be born from Mary (The African-American community).

Understanding powerful and prophetic concept is a necessary to appreciate its true value. It begins with the words Virgin and Immaculate.

Immaculate actually means without spot or blemish. It is a word that defines flawlessness or without error. For something to be unusually clean and without blemish or flaw, it is said to be immaculate. This defines a condition of innocence.

Whereas, miraculous is the nature of a miracle: an extraordinary event manifesting divine intervention in human affairs. Connecting these two terms with conception it is commonly thought of as the act of a female becoming pregnant without a male to impregnate her. However, conception has broader meaning that refers to the original, beginning, start or formation of any entity including a thought or idea.

More importantly, it is the capacity, function, process of forming or understanding ideas or abstractions and their symbols. In essence, conception is the complex product of reflective or abstract thinking. To that end, it becomes increasingly clear that we are dealing with the mind; especially, considering that conception comes from the word "concept" which means something conceived in the mind such as an idea, thought, design, plan or intention.

As to the event, although classifying it as a miracle, may be a great deal to handle, however, having been nurtured in a community that was just up from slavery, and a nationalistic and to some extent a racist movement, it gives the impression that these terms are best define the phenomenon of Imam Mohammed receiving the concept. A concept that was vastly different than the ones he was taught. This is an issue easily resolved by simply examining its inception.

Surah Al Mu'minin of the Qur'an in Ayah **50,** Allah says, "And We made the son of Mary and his mother as a Sign." To appreciate social evolution, it is most crucial to understand scripture; in that, a great deal of prophecy and scriptural language are symbols and metaphors, and address a time in their future which may be our present. It is imperative to have an open mind as the means to solve the implied meanings. At the same time as it is very important not to step too far away from principles; however, to be aware of abstract concept, it is necessary to contemplate the possibilities, and the different arguments that are presented in this type of format in order to reach the logical conclusion. Practically, it is the same as peeling away the skin of a Pomegranate to get to the sweet delicious seeds of its core.

Ideas, philosophies, concepts and sometimes thoughts and suggestions are presented by physical images such as plants and other objects in the physical creation; the most common are male and female images. The images are used to depict a particular characteristic or nature; it is that characteristic or nature that gives meaning to the story or picture.

In real life, the man carries the sperm and a woman receives and gives birth to it. Therefore, in scriptural symbolic language, the Father represents the entity that is the carrier of the philosophy or concept (the Sperm) and the mother is the group or community in who the concept takes root and grows.

Consequently, son or daughter represent that the idea has taken root and born as a new society. These symbols are used to help us to understand how human societies evolve.

While many cultures and civilizations have stories of a virgin giving birth to a son, there are none so descriptive and rich with symbols and metaphors then the one presented in the Qur'an and Bible.

The Bible captures this event in the Old (Torah, the Jewish holy book) and New Testament. The Old and New Testament are into one holy book of the Christians called The Holy Bible. First the Torah or Old Testament, in the book of Isaiah, chapter 1, verse 14, "Therefore the Lord himself shall give you a sign; a virgin shall conceive, and bear a son, and shall call his name Immanuel." In that language, Immanuel means that G-d is with us. Second the New Testament, in Luke, chapter 1, verses 30, 31 and 34, the same prophecy is made. "And the angel said unto her, Fear not, Mary; for thou hast found favour with God," reads verse 30. Verse 31 says, "And, behold, thou shalt conceive in thy womb, and brings forth a son, and shalt call his name JE'SUS." Concluding in 34, "Then said Mary unto the angel, how shall this be, seeing I know not a man?" This last verse verifies that Mary is a virgin. Furthermore, the Old and New Testament are proof that the Jewish community and Christians have the same Prophecy. Although these accounts in the Bible are the same, we will utilize the version in the Qur'an because the Arabic words give a broader view.

Suratah 3 Al-I'Imran   Ayah 45

مَرْيَمَ وَمَا كُنتَ لَدَيْهِمْ إِذْ يَخْتَصِمُونَ ۝ إِذْ قَالَتِ ٱلْمَلَٰٓئِكَةُ يَٰمَرْيَمُ إِنَّ ٱللَّهَ يُبَشِّرُكِ بِكَلِمَةٍ مِّنْهُ ٱسْمُهُ ٱلْمَسِيحُ عِيسَى ٱبْنُ مَرْيَمَ وَجِيهًا فِى ٱلدُّنْيَا وَٱلْءَاخِرَةِ وَمِنَ ٱلْمُقَرَّبِينَ ۝

Yusuf Ali   "Behold! The angels said 'O Mary! Allah giveth thee glad tidings of a Word from Him: his name will be Christ Jesus the son of Mary held in honor in this world and the Hereafter and of (the company of) those nearest to Allah.'"

Pickthall   "(And remember) when the angels said: O Mary! Allah giveth thee glad tidings of a word from Him, whose name is the Messiah, Jesus, son of Mary, illustrious in the world and the Hereafter, and one of those brought near (unto Allah)."

Ayah 46

Yusuf Ali   "He shall speak to the people in childhood and in maturity and he shall be (of the company) of the righteous."

Pickthall   "He will speak unto mankind in his cradle and in his manhood, and he is of the righteous."

Transliteration Wa yukallimun na_sa fil mahdi wa kahlaw wa minas sa_lihin (a).

قَالَتْ رَبِّ أَنَّىٰ يَكُونُ لِى وَلَدٌ وَلَمْ يَمْسَسْنِى بَشَرٌ قَالَ كَذَٰلِكِ ٱللَّهُ يَخْلُقُ مَا يَشَآءُ إِذَا قَضَىٰٓ أَمْرًا فَإِنَّمَا يَقُولُ لَهُۥ كُن فَيَكُونُ ﴿٤٧﴾

Ayah 47

She said: "O my Lord! how shall I have a son when no man hath touched me?" He said: "Even so: Allah createth what He willeth; when He hath decreed a plan He but saith to it `Be' and it is!

It is clear that Qur'an and Bible address this issue thoroughly, and with the same implied meaning. It was on the meaning of this subject, around the late 1970's, that some of Imam Muhammed's followers took issue. They viewed this example literally (word for word). They could not understand the implied meanings in this Ayahs and verses. However, not to discourage them, Imam Muhammad explained that it is important to follow the spirit as well as the letter of the Qur'an. As students of Qur'an, Bible and Imam Muhammed, we must recognize that Allah revealed scripture on levels that are understood according to the sincerity, open mindedness and intellectual comprehension of the person studying it.

This is a Miracle that uses people and individuals as types to address a broader concern or matter. It must be understood that the reality includes all humanity; it is not just a story of individuals in the pages of history.

First, we must understand that these concepts in scripture are pictures that Allah is presenting with a meaning in them. Second, we must understand the meaning of the picture, then and only then, will we get the true significance by Allah's permission. For this reason, a language is needed to crystallize those concepts.

It would be done in three stages the similar manner as the physical birth of a child (the zygote, embryo and fetus). It, the first stage, began with introduction of a new and powerful knowledge to the African-American community in a depressed area of Detroit, Michigan some 80 years ago.

CHAPTER 12

IMPREGNATING THE VIRGIN

It was sometime in the year 1964, when a small, soft spoken and humble man of the African-American community made radio broadcast to his followers and the listening audience. He began his talk in these words, "Greetings to you, I am The Honorable Elijah Muhammad, The Preacher of Freedom, Justice and Equality to the so-called American Negro. Not a Negro, but the Lost and Found Members of a Great Nation, the Asiatic Black Nation from the Tribe of Shabazz." Immediately, he established a positive self image of the African-America community as he emphasized his purpose.

Simultaneously, after introducing himself, he began to bring into the light his mentor and teacher in these words, " We have been lost from our own kind and from our country, for the past 400 years until the coming of Almighty God, in the Person of Master Fard Muhammad in 1930, July the 4th. It was around the spring of 1931 when that he made himself known to us." After referring to Fard as Almighty G-d in person, he spoke how Fard made himself known to our community as he stated, "He got among us, by taking orders for made-to-measure suits for men folks. And He finally began to teach those who would take an order from Him. That was a very slow progress that He was making at that time, until that He began to get acquainted with more and more of our people." However, slow the process, you can see that this was the beginning of the impregnation of the African-American people.

This indicates that as a sperm unites with the egg to become a zygote so did Fard put his concept into the minds of selected few while building them into a special social group. His hope was to impregnate at least one mind to perpetuate his theory. His impact on the African-American community was not only historical, it was biblical in nature.

As The Honorable Elijah Muhammad continued to talk, it became very clear that because his father was a Baptist Preacher, he had knowledge of the scripture. He made some religious connections as he said, "And finally I happened to get to him. And when I saw Him, I said to Him, myself, after looking at Him, it came to me that this is The Man that the Scripture prophesied of that would come in the Last Day, called the second-coming of Jesus or The Son of Man or God in Person." As profound as it may be, Fard needed someone with some scriptural knowledge as well as commitment.

112

"So, I made my way to Him," Elijah continued, "and I'd taken Him by the hand. He shook hands with me. And I told him, I said, you are the one that the Bible prophesied of that would come in The Last Days, the second-coming of Jesus. And some is sent to be the Son of Man. And as I spoke to Him, He says to me in my ear, 'Yes, I am He that they have been looking to see for the last 2,000 years, but who else knows that. You are the only one that knows it. So keep quiet.' He ordered me to keep quiet." This was what they both wanted, the moment of solidarity; the sperm and the egg united as one. Elijah needed a savior; Fard needed a devoted loyal student, one who would dedicate himself to carry out his plan.

So, for the next two or three years Fard refused to allow The Honorable Elijah Muhammad to preach to the people that he was The One. Elijah had to wait until Fard was no more among their community then he could tell the people what he wanted to of Him. "So this went on for a time," Elijah said, "And today, after about 32 years, the Truth of this Mighty One, the Long-looked-for-to-come All Mighty God, IN PERSON!"

This speech of The Honorable Elijah Muhammad introduced two men that may have had different motivations. However, the historical impact they would have on the African-American community and subsequently the world would be astronomical. The challenge they faced was enormous in the fact they would have to reverse the psychological mind-set of an entire community or at the very least, a sizable amount to respond.

In 1930, one year after the death of Noble Drew Ali, America was still segregated. In the South, there were two laws; one for Caucasian Americans and one for African-Americans. Separate school systems, residential communities and public facilities were throughout the South and in many Northern States. All through the country, many African-Americans were poor and suffering with no jobs or jobs with very little pay. The beating, lynching and torture of them were frequent and seemingly legal. The concept of freedom, justice and equality was truly lacking for African-Americans in America.

Although some African-American individuals and organizations formed to combat it, "White Supremacy" dominated the social atmosphere to the point that it created a state of Black inferiority complex in most African-Americans. Some of them would try to escape by bleaching their skin and straighten their hair...they did not want to be an African-American. The history of the physical and mental abuse of the African-American community is well documented; more important, because others have tried and some were still trying, it is important to understand that the change that The Honorable Elijah Muhammad and Fard Muhammad were looking for was difficult to achieve.

Fard was no stranger in America. Here, he had to learn America and study the habits of the African-American most of whom had not completed an elementary education. He had arrived in America several years before he made himself known; some records indicate that he had stayed in America for more than twenty years studying the habits of America as well as the African-American people.

He had the opportunity to study the effect of the concepts and movements of the African-American as they battled "white supremacy." He had the chance to study men such as Garvey with his concept of separatism and nationhood; Father Divine who taught the Black man was G-d concept; most important, Drew Ali who taught that there was a connection between the African-American and Moorish ancestry that was hidden from them. Fard even had the use of Darwinism.

He stayed in England for some time, just before returning to America. Originally, he was from near

Lahore, India (Pakistan). There he belonged to the Ahmadiyyah movement; an Islamic group that with some strange beliefs that allowed Fard to take on the guise of G-d in his purpose of freeing men. He was frustrated with them. He also was disguised with "white supremacy" and ignorance in the Islamic leadership. Added to this, he did not like the British rule. By the time he got to America, he had a few things to prove to himself and a few other groups and people.

He was known by several names, most notably Professor or Master Fard. These were titles used by teachers in the British Empire school systems. He taught high school in Pakistan. He also used W.F. Fard, Wali Fard, and Fard Muhammad. By cloaking himself, he was able to move around undetected in his real identity.

His true identity, as explained by Imam W. D. Mohammed was Muhammad Abdullah. He consulted with Imam Mohammed in Philadelphia prior to Imam Mohammed becoming leader of the Nation of Islam. Regardless of which name he used, the scheme and its design he had produced to supplant "white supremacy" in the psychic of African-American was masterful.

In 1930, one year after the death of Noble Drew Ali, Fard began his work—the methodology of the destruction of "white supremacy." He planned to draw on a part of an uneducated or barely educated African-American population and educate them in a knowledge that had the resemblance supreme intellectual authority. This information, once acted upon, would improve the physical, economical, psychological appearance and behavior of African-Americans. His lessons had names such as Supreme Wisdom and the Actual Facts...there was a magnetic quality to them. These lessons were similar in presentation as Drew Ali's Seven Circle lessons.

But, Fard did something that was drastically different from other freedom fighters; He dropped a bomb in mental fabric of America that exploded like loud noise, shattering hidden myth of "white supremacy." He taught that the Caucasians were a race of devil; created to do evil and spread mischief in the world. He said they were born devils and could not change.

In the Actual Facts and lessons, he posed some powerful questions and answers that each member had to commit to memory. For instance, "Who is the Original Man?" Answer, "The Original Man is the Asiatic Black Man, The Maker, The Owner, The Cream of Planet Earth, and God the Universe." This method is called rote memorization. It is not designed to teach critical or analytical thinking: it is fast method to prepare a student to commit something to memory as instructed by the teacher. It is the way we learn the alphabets as a child.

In theory, it was designed to connect the so-called Negro to a more positive image of themselves and their situation: the self esteem and pride is immediately established in the African-American community.

The second question continued to build on the self-image of the African-American while bringing down the image of the Caucasian- American. It stated, "Who is the Colored Man?" Answer, "The Colored Man is the Caucasian-White Man, Yocub's grafted Devil, Skunk of the Planet Earth." This hit America like a nuclear bomb. The psychology began the change.

He brought the image of the Caucasian off its high perch to a low creature...it amounted to character assassination. It made Caucasian-America evaluate themselves and rethink their position. These two Actual Facts were only a few of the many question and answer scenarios developed by Fard.

He developed myth that could only be traced back to him for authenticity of its reality or origin. He skillfully prepared lessons. They began with an explanation that the Asiatic Black Man created himself; and then, he created the earth as his home. He was the god and owner of the earth; but, no individual gods who live forever. Their wisdom and work may live six thousand or twenty-five thousand years, but the actual individual may have died within a hundred or two hundred years. The longest one would live was around a thousand years. There is no God Living who was here in the Creation of the Universe, but they produce Gods from them and Their Wisdom lives in the people.

Fard's explanation of how the moon came into existence was based on the idea that one of the Asiatic Black Men who was a scientist got angry and packed dynamite into the earth and set off the charge. According to Fard's lessons, the scientist was trying to destroy the earth, but failed. He only cracked it, and the smaller part flowed out in space, but could not get out of earth's gravitational pull so it orbits the earth. Make no mistake; Fard was not a foolish or irrational man. There may have been deeper meanings in his lessons. For example, in religious language, the moon can be symbolic of a prophet and his community. A prophet comes from his own kind, and like the moon reflexes the light of the sun to the earth, he reflexes the truth from the Creator to the community.

While not condoning fables as a way of establishing truth, we must marvel at how Fard planned to change the dietary habits of the African-American and forbid the eating of pork. In this myth, an Asiatic Black Man, a scientist, wanted to clean up the earth of its filth, dead matter and garbage. He took the cat and rat, and crossed it with a dog because of its size, he came up with the pig, hog or wild boar to eat the filth of the earth. This animal was deemed as unclean and not fit for human consumption. Fard emphasized that it is the foulest animal. It lives off nothing but filth. The only way to get it to live and eat better food was to keep him from getting to filth. It is 99 per cent poisonous...it can hardly be poisoned with other poison such as lye. Snakes can't poison them; they eat them and fatten. The bite of the snakes doesn't harm them, because they would eat the biter. He is so poisonous and filthy, that nature had to prepare him a sewer line and you may find the opening on his forelegs...it is a little hole out of which oozes pus. This is because the filth of his body that cannot be passed fast enough.

He is the greediest animal. He never knows or cares to stop eating, as long as he sees something to eat. He is the dumbest animal. He keeps his nose smelling and eyes looking for something in the earth. He can be fed all day long, and he will never look up to see his feeder.

In case of bad weather arising, he is never intelligent enough to go in before it actually starts raining or hailing on his back. He takes no warning. He will keep his head in the earth, rooting until the storm is lashing his back with rain and the lighting is blinding his eyes.

Fard's dietary plan encouraged them to learn to eat one meal a day, and let it be without swine flesh and many of the ailments and sufferings would disappear. He had a cure for the DIABETICS: Eat one meal a day, and lay off that starch and sugar that is causes the sickness.

This too has a ring of cleverness. For example, a bad or seemingly evil person may do some good or help someone else, but, it is not recommended that anyone should develop or take up their bad habits or way of life.

Yocub's grafted Devil was one Fard's fascinating myth about the big headed scientist, Yocub. It was this man who grafted the so-called White Man. When he was a little boy, playing with two pieces of metal, he found that the opposite ends were attached to each other, while the same ends repelled each other. So, he went and told his mother that he was going to create a people when he grows up.

As a man, He began his experiment on the Island of Patmos. His idea was to mate the people according to the color of their skin; the light complexion with the light complexion for period of six hundred years. This will produce a lighter complexion of people.

In the first two hundred years, he got the Japanese people. In the second two hundred years, he got the Chinese people; and in the last two, he got the Caucasian people. According to the story, because all the good was grafted out of them, they caused so much trouble with the Original Man; they had to be roped off in the Caucasus Mountain range. This is where they got the name, from the mountains; the place they were rope in was called Europe (we rope you in). As farfetched as this may seem, World War II was fought over the concept that one side thought it was a divine race, Nazi Germany. They also thought the Jews were inherently evil and corrupted the rest of humanity.

Fard was dealing with the core of racism. His plan was actually Darwinism in reverse. Instead of strong mating the strong to produce a superior race as the concept of selective breeding, Fard taught that the Asiatic Black Man started strong as a G-d, and grafted a segment of his population to become weak and evil— the Caucasian as a race of devils.

After putting his scheme and lessons together, Fard arrived in Detroit around 1931 and immediately established his plan. After winning the confidence of some of the African-Americas, he formed the Nation of Islam. They were a highly disciplined organization...meetings were held at 3408 Hastings Street on the top floor in an old theater. His plan was to shape the minds of the members to an independent way of thinking that would lead to a unique analysis of the Qur'an. He would teach his members for five to six hours in one session. The Honorable Elijah Muhammad, who was given the surname "Kareem," was a member of his minister's class.

As to the work of Fard, Imam Mohammed explains it by saying, "The WCIW began with the teachings of this man. In his own symbolic way, using symbolic and mystical teachings, he added the teachings of black-nationalism to the teachings the original man (the birth of Adam). With it, he put "black" on the original man and took "white" off of the original man, making the original man black and making the Caucasian so-called white man not original. He reversed the psychology and with it he brought us to practice Islam in our lives...The decent dress and Islamic mentality served to revive Islam in the West. But this revival was a revival in mental discipline, moral discipline, and physical discipline. It did not concern itself too much with spiritual revival or spiritual discipline. Instead of beginning as prophet Muhammad (PBUH) began- by calling the people's attention to the reality that there is one G-d and that that G-d is Creator and all else is creation, Fard Muhammad overlooked the importance of that and put his stress on material discipline (physical discipline)....His teachings accomplished the revitalizing of Islam and the revival of Islam in our physical life."

During the early 30's, The Nation of Islam's membership grew to approximately 25,000 under Fard's leadership. He established three Temples: Temple No. 1(Detroit), Temple No. 2 (Chicago), and Temple No. 3 (Milwaukee). Shortly after that, in 1933, with the seed of a new community firmly planted, impregnating the African-American community, he disappeared from Detroit leaving the budding Nation of Islam awaiting fertilization in the hand of his first minister, The Honorable Elijah Muhammad.

CHAPTER 13

CLINGING CLOT

As an embryo grows in the woman, to the necked eye, you cannot tell if it is a boy or girl in the mother, but you know there is something in there. For forty years, the embryo (Nation of Islam) was growing in the African-American community. It had attracted the attention of nations and people over the world, especially those in America. They knew something was growing in the African-American community. They did know what it was.

Some said it was a religious group called the Black Muslims; others thought it was a nationalist organization teaching Black pride and they wanted some land to establish a nation of their own inside America; some felt it was a racist movement proclaiming the white man as a race of devils.

In one of his speeches, The Honorable Elijah Muhammad said, "We are living in an evil time and in a time of great trouble and a time of the threat of universal destruction of nations. The so-called Negro, The Lost and Found Members of a Mighty Nation, must know the truth. They have been deprived of the knowledge of self and others. The greatest work that we must do, according to the Mission that All Mighty God, in the Person of Master Fard Muhammad, gave to me it is to make known the poor Lost and Found members of the Black Nation the True knowledge of self, their history, and the knowledge of their slave-master, and the history of their slave-master and the work of their slave-master, the creation of their slave-master and the nature of their slave-master." Although this speech was made later in the career of the Honorable Elijah Muhammad, it is clear that the philosophy by Fard had taken root and the embryo was growing.

Ironically, just a few years prior, the Honorable Elijah Muhammad like so many African-Americans of the times was hopelessly lost. Occasionally, they would turn to alcohol to relieve the pain of their social and economic reality...it was during the time of the Great Depression in the 1930's. He, like many of his contemporaries, was in a repetitive life of joblessness with a hungry family of four young children and a wife. His resurrection had to be the first miracle for the mission to succeed.

The Honorable Elijah Muhammad was born Elijah Poole in a small community near Sandersville, Georgia in October 1897. William and Marie Poole, his parents, were sharecroppers. When Elijah was six his father, who was also a Baptist preacher, moved the family to Cordele.

At the age of 18, in 1915, Elijah met his future wife and partner in the upcoming social changes in America, Clara Evans. She too was born in Georgia two years after him on November 2, 1899. They were married on May 2, 1917, and four years later, they moved to Macon where their first son was born. He worked in a local mill and rose to the level of foreman.

By 1923, Elijah and Clara along with two children, his parents, brothers and sisters moved to Hamtramck, Michigan. He found work at American Can Company and Chevrolet. Again, as in the Macon mills, he rose to leadership role in these factories. However, the family was on the move, they migrated to the big city of Detroit

Detroit was not to gracious, Elijah and his family had a tough time finding and holding work. There he moved from job to job and had a difficult time caring for his family...by this time, they had three more children. The Great Depression in the 1930's gritted the country with joblessness, bread lines, and despair, Detroit and Elijah were no exceptions. In the same year, Clara heard from a friend of a mysterious silk peddler by the name of Fard

Muhammad, and he was teaching something that she might be interested in. Eventually, in 1931, she took her husband to hear and meet him. This was the very same meeting that the Honorable Elijah Muhammad described on his radio broadcast in 1964. After the meeting, Elijah had Clara to get rid of all the pork in their house.

Upon embracing the teaching of Fard Muhammad, they were taught how to prepare food and how to follow the teaching of the Nation of Islam. Elijah was given the surname "Karriem" and his wife was Sister Clara. They completed their family with eight children with Wallace being the seventh of the eight. Subsequent to that, leaving Elijah as the leader, acknowledged by the followers, Fard left Detroit to mysteriously reappear in the 1950's as Muhammad Abdullah; however, following his departure from Detroit, opposition within the community threatened Elijah's leadership and his life.

The Honorable Elijah Muhammad and his family moved to Chicago in September 1934. He continued the work of Fard, and completed the establishment of Temple # 2 in Chicago. With his family in the capable hands of his wife Sister Clara, he was on the run from the mid 30's to the early 40's. While in hiding, he was spreading the message and establishing new temples throughout

America. As the Nation of Islam was growing in membership, it was also attracting the authorities. As a result, by May of 1942, at age 45, he was arrested by the Federal Bureau of Investigation for draft evasion. While technically he was beyond the drafting age, he was imprisoned at the Federal Corrections Institution in Milan, Michigan until his release in 1946.

Meanwhile, those years he was imprisoned and on the run, it was the intelligent, courageous Sister Clara Muhammad the kept her family and the Nation of Islam together. The Honorable Elijah Muhammad would send letters, and she would communicate to rest of the followers. Her efforts were as great as any heroine in the history of America. Her ability and commitment to the movement was unparalleled. Mary Bethune and Eleanor Roosevelt are women whose stature would rival hers. While she was holding the community, Elijah was developing a philosophy that shook the nation.

While maintaining the values taught to him by Fard, upon his release, the Honorable Elijah Muhammad's message of "Do for self" caught fire in the African-American community. The idea of building a black nation independent of the white people attracted thousands of African-Americans, especially the younger generation. Among them was a fiery, intelligent and loyal disciples namely, Malcolm X and perhaps the most famous person on the planet, Muhammad Ali the heavyweight boxing champion of the World.

With their assistance and others like them, the Nation of Islam grew at an alarming rate. It had grown to over 75 temples and hundreds of thousands of loyal followers. By the time the Honorable Elijah Muhammad passed at the age of 78 in 1975, with no aid from white people, he, according to some reports, built and left behind an empire estimated to be worth between eight and sixty million dollars. It included land and cattle holdings in Michigan, Georgia and Alabama. In addition, there were grocery stores, restaurants, mosques, schools, newspapers, homes, clothing stores and a materially flourishing Nation of Islam throughout America.

Paralleling the economic growth of its mother, the African-American community, the sperm planted by Fard Muhammad had united with egg or mind of the Honorable Elijah Muhammad and as an embryo it was now ready in the form of a fetus that has all its features and organs in place. In other words, it was time for someone from the Nation of Islam to form a better and clear direction to the plan of Allah. In essence, he had to break out of the darkness of its mother's womb (the lessons of Fard and religious symbolism) into the light of The Holy Qur'an to embrace Al-Islam as establish by Prophet Muhammed Ibn Abdullah.

Spirit of Bilal

CHAPTER 14

CHOOSING ONE

Like the unborn fetus, this community had to take the shape and form it would have to face the world for the first time with an identity of its own. Clinging to the philosophy of the Nation of Islam as its umbilical cord, it had to be preparing for cutting away of those symbols and metaphors that held it so tightly to its nationalistic ideology; it had to get ready to breathe for itself. It had to take on a new way of thinking and viewing the world that it was about to enter for the first time. It had to come into a new mindset, a grooming that began with Imam W. D. Mohammad.

After the passing of the Honorable Elijah Muhammad, in 1975, his son Wallace D. Mohammed became the leader of the Nation of Islam. Prior to the passing of his father, Wallace had done an extensive study of the Arabic language, the Qur'an, the Bible, the language of Fard and the work of his father. Even though, he grew up in a very rigid environment and organization under the leadership of his father, The Honorable Elijah Muhammad, he was encouraged to be a free thinker and have an open mind.

As a child, he had a scientific approach toward learning, childhood curiosities, and sincerity. Certainly, the fact that he was supported and loved by family and friends played a powerful role in his success as an adult.

Insightfully, it was Professor Diab, his Arabic instructor, who mentioned that his younger brother Akbar was the best Arabic student, but noticed that young Wallace was the best translator. This was an early indication that Imam Mohammed had the ability to handle concepts and analytical situations. While still a junior FOI, an instructor wanted someone to come before the class and give a talk, it was the young Wallace that was selected. As an adult, he appreciated the idea of digging deep into theories, beliefs, thoughts and notions with a different view. Many times this required him to review tons of material; religious or secular.

He became a minister in the Nation of Islam under his father, the aging Honorable Elijah Muhammad. One evening, Imam Mohammed recalled, at his father's dinner table, someone produced a tape of Minister Wallace's thoughts he revealed on a radio show in Indiana on the "Mythological gods is the burden on the American people." The tape began to play, his father who was weak from an illness listened, and then suddenly he jumped up at the table and said, "My son's got it!"   "My son's got it!"   From that moment on, Wallace was allowed to preach any where he wanted, and he could say whatever he chose.

Consequently, his keen insight was recognized and became more obvious to those that were around him. By the time, the Honorable Elijah Muhammad had passed, to the leaders of the Nation of Islam, although he was still a young man, Wallace was their choice to lead the Nation.

Spirit of Bilal

CHAPTER 15

BREATHING PURE LIFE

The birth of the community began with Imam Mohammed as he developed a disposition that allowed him to acknowledge and understand the thoughts and direction in which Allah would guide him even if it did not always agree with other opinions coming from inside or outside of his community. His trust was rewarded as he began to formulate ideas and information that shone as a brilliant light out of darkness. He expressed it as understanding the Divine Word.

As a consequence, for his efforts, Allah blessed him to develop a unique insight; in essence, a new language. This is no ordinary language such as French, English or Arabic, it was a language of concepts that unlocked and decoded religious and secular belief systems.

This Understanding was an evolutionary perspective on the religious message from the Creator that was far in advanced to other scholars and what they had to offer in this era. It would prove to be a contemporary insight of religious knowledge and understanding—his Tafsir.

This would uniquely identify him and the community he would deliver.

With guidance of Allah, Imam Mohammed freed himself from the philosophy of Fard and embraced Al-Islam as expressed in the Qur'an. The Qur'an brought him into the light of understanding that freed him and the thousands of members of the Nation of Islam who understood him, and had the trust and faith to follow this new mindset. To free the community from the womb of knowledge they were in, was neither an easy task nor could it be done overnight.

As he began to transform the community, Imam Mohammed focused on saving the precious crop (followers of the Honorable Elijah Muhammad) as a primary goal; however, even more so, his secondary goal was to prepare them for community life in Al-Islam as expressed in the Qur'an, and the Life Example of Prophet Muhammed Ibn Abdullah. With this focus, it was inevitable that he had to destroy racism in all its forms. He knew that this community had to free itself of black supremacy and racism in order to take on the responsibility of calling the world to Human Excellence.

Imam Mohammed announced to the followers to Remake the World. What kind of world...the kind of a world that only Al Rahman (Attribute of Allah) could make. In an article "Deliverance From The Womb," in the book, Teachings of WD Muhammad, Imam Mohammed stated, "The work of 'Al Rahman' suggests many things to us that are like the work of a father. It is to bring about a Divine creation in the moral nature of the man, his righteousness, high principles of conduct, excellence of character, and the dignified mind that lifts the man above petty, unclean, and ignorant things."

"The earth," he continued, "cannot create this kind of being. It takes the work of Allah, a reunion with the Divine Source. This converting back to the Divine Nature comes from the Power of Divine Being." Having this knowledge, Imam Mohammed had to begin his work of Remaking the World by first remaking the world in the minds of his followers.

The mind of the followers that he inherited was a world wherein Fard was Allah in Person, and the Honorable Elijah Muhammad was his Messenger; the Black Man was the God and Owner of the earth (The Original Man), and the White Man was Yocub's grafted Devil.

Elijah's job was to free or raise what they called the mentally dead so-called Negro who had been stripped of the knowledge of themselves, and had a state of mind filled with white supremacy and racism. Fard's plan worked in the hands of his student, The Honorable

Elijah Muhammad. They reverse that process of white supremacy in the mind of the community.

The African-Americans began to love themselves, cleanup their communities, build family relationships, and establish businesses. This was a great accomplishment save for that, it left followers with the belief in a false god in the person of Master Fard and in the mindset of black supremacy, racism. It was a way of life that the people loved and respected as being genuine; a world created in their minds. Unknowingly, as they clung to black supremacy, they were in the state of an unborn child dying in its mother's womb, ready to be stillborn.

To change this world in the minds of members of the Nation of Islam required compassion and a complete understanding of what had to be done and how fragile the situation. Before the birth of a newborn baby, it must be completely shaped into what it will be when it enters the world. Imam Mohammed had a delicate task to perform in addition to selecting a direction for the community. He was confronted with several options.

He could have directed the momentum of the group to be like the Moorish American organization. They had a direction for the African-American and they practice Al-Islam according to their understanding.

There were other much smaller groups such as the Black Israelites or the Hamitic Arabs philosophy that was introduced by Professor Muhammad Ezaldeen. At the time, it also seemed logical to maintain the ideology of the Nation of Islam, and stay on that path.

However, the one aspect that these organizations had in common was that they had the same problem that plagued the Jewish faith.

They are saddled with a problem that is essentially racist...not necessary the type that practices discrimination against other groups, but in the sense that they are born divine at the moment they come into the world—a superiority complex over others not of their linage—this is inherent with their belief.

Just as the Jewish faith, their belief system is based on a lukewarm ancestral worship. Their qualification to righteousness was their bloodline. The Jews, for example, can be defined as a matriarch in terms of what qualifies one to be a Jew—to be born of Jewish mother. Although a true Matriarch is a woman who is recognized as being the head of a family, community, or people, the link is in their practice.

This practice stems back to Sarah the wife of Prophet Abraham. Although G-d never made a promise to Sarah about her offspring, it is this event on which they hang their destiny. The scripture is very clear that the promise was made to Abraham.

Abraham had one son named Isaac by Sarah, and the other named Ishmail by Hagar; Both Isaac and Ishmail would qualify. In this matter, there is no question because the Arabs and Jews would have the same problem if they claim divinity by way of the bloodline...they would be entering a subtle form of racism (superiority complex). In fact, it is a situation that they should not have because the prophecy actually says Abraham's offsprings are those who believe as Abraham believes. With a little understanding, it is clear that this issue is about faith and not bloodline.

However, as to the Jewish people, the proper term is an ethno-religious group. According to Wikipedia, "Ethno-religious communities define their ethnic identity neither exclusively by ancestral heritage nor simply by religious affiliation, but often through a combination of both; either a common geographical origin, or descent from a small number of common ancestors." The Wikipedia continued,"In an ethno-religious group, particular emphasis is placed upon religious endogamy, and the concurrent discouragement of interfaith marriages or intercourse, as a means of preserving the stability and historical longevity of the community and culture." It is clear that this presents a problem because religious endogamy can be tied to ethnic nationalism if the ethno-religious group possesses a historical base in a specific region or land.

Overall, many religions have this problem in one form or another...it is more pronounced in those that tie race, ethnic group or a label to their divine right as projected by a deity. Whether they are called The Nation of Islam, Jews, Black Israelites, Moorish Americans, Hamitic Arabs, Shias, Ahmadiyyah, Sunni, Hannafi or any label that defines its group by definition to be better than others, they are a form of an ethno-religious group or ancestral worship; their divinity is connected first and foremost to labels, bloodline or ancestry rather than faith or conduct.

While discussing the issue ethno-religious group as it relates to that group pretending to be the savior or redeemer of humanity, Imam Mohammed was clear when he stated, "It makes it clear that it is the truth from Allah that the man or group passes on that redeems humanity. The idea of a man being a Savior plays into Satan's Scheme."

He continued, "Satan wants for us all to claim that we are divine over our fellow human beings simply by birth or indoctrination. Every time one of us thinks that our race or group is better than the other people of earth Satan encourages that thought. Allah says, 'We are judged by our conduct. Our best dress is our conduct.'"

"The idea of a divine or chosen race as a birth right is far off course," concluded Imam Mohammed.

This signals that the world of tomorrow will not be built on racism or groups with a hint self ordained supremacy. Obviously, all forms of racism and organizations that depend on any of those forms are dead. It is just a matter of time.

Knowing the history of the different religions and groups and having acute understanding of the pitfalls and poison of racism, Imam Mohammed chose to call himself Muslim in accordance with the Qur'an and the example set by Prophet Muhammed. Muslim is not preceded by any other word such as Black, Moorish, Sunni, Hannafi, Shi'a or any other prefix. Allah did not do it in the Qur'an, nor did the Prophet give a prefix to Muslim. The word Muslim means submission to Allah or the nature in which He Created the human being. He asks no more than that, complete submission. A Muslim should be all the righteous characteristics in one.

Anything else is an addition made by man in his weaken mental state.

Imam Mohammed chose Muslim, the Qur'an, life example of Prophet Muhammed (PBUH) and trusted that Allah would guide him in the correct understanding.

Consequently, he had to go into the mind of the followers and correct a philosophy that they had become comfortable with. He was to face a situation that was very similar if not the same as in Ancient Egypt where the Pharaoh ruled as a god/ king.

After getting free of white supremacy, unaware of actual episode; the followers in the Nation of Islam were in a world that was the same as the world pictured in the Qur'an about Ancient Egypt. In Ancient Egypt, Allah sent Moses to free Hebrews from the physical bondage of Pharaoh. He instructed Moses to tell Pharaoh "To Let My People Go." Similarly, Imam Mohammed had to free the minds of the people in the Nation of Islam from mental bondage; Fard's lessons and melodramatic concepts of reality was holding their minds in confinement in the same way as Pharaoh held the Hebrews in captivity.

Imam Mohammed proceeded to cut the psychological umbilical cord by explaining that the concept of Adam was about the birth of human intellect that was above all other creations. The physical body of the human being was formed as a conduit for the rational mind; In essence, "Man Means Mind."

He continued to reach into their minds as he taught, "The Original Man (original mind) developed naturally out of creation from its contact and its involvement with creation." As the followers became believers, he expounded, "The mind developed and grew naturally in the physical creation designed by G-d to bring the natural growth of the mind." As he brought the old form of thinking to a close and opened a new window for light, he stated, "That mind is the Original Man."

He followed this up with the knowledge of the devil. He posed the question, "Who is Satan, the devil?

Over the history of humanity, many people have concocted some supernatural concepts regarding the devil. Imam Mohammed explained that situation in these words, "Many religious people have been spooked up on the churches, the synagogues and the mosques and made to think that Satan is some invisible ghost that hovers around, waiting for an opportunity to come and take over your life and lead you to do something bad." He followed this with, "If there is a devil in you, that devil has grown in you."

From the focus narrows and the picture starts to clear as he states, "It has come to birth on something that started within you like lies, weak ideas, or wrong thinking." He taught them the plain truth without the nursery rhymes. The devil originates from within the human mind that is corrupted by wrong thinking because Allah did not create the devil or Satan (Shaytan). Allah created Lucifer in the Bible and the Jinn in the Qur'an, and both of them were created to serve Allah. "The Jinn" Allah says in the Qur'an, "He Created him from fire." It is clearly explained in the Qur'an that the Jinn became Iblis (an arrogant Jinn), then an enemy to man as Shaytan (devil). This indicates how the Jinn can degenerate into Satan. It all begins with lies, weak ideas or wrong thinking that you allow to influence you.

"These things begin to grow a particular disposition in you and pretty soon your disposition is one of evil and wickedness. If they continue to grow, you will take the form of a devil," stated Imam Mohammed. The picture is clear that the human mind is the frontier. It is where the battle between good and evil is staged, and then it spills out onto the earth. Most important, there is a remedy to the destruction of the devil. That which will destroy the devil is the truth...the Divine Truth and Knowledge. In scripture, it is call the "Lake of Fire." Allah tells us in the Qur'an the Shaytan doesn't haxe any power over the human being by causing Shaytan to say again that he, Shaytan, is not man's Lord, he only called and the human being came.

As Imam Mohammed broke down the meanings of Fard's lessons while defining concepts in the religious language of the world, he was developing a new insight into the concepts. This insight opened the door for a better understanding of scripture. It made clear and understandable the scheme of Fard.

Simultaneously, by unlocking the concept of religion and other intricate concepts in the Qur'an, Bible and other religious text, he, with his insight, elevated the thinking of his followers to scrutinize in depth the concepts in religion. He encouraged them to use rational thought by following concepts and ideas to their logical conclusion. In other words, conclusions and ideas are based on facts, clear rational thought, and sensible reasoning.

The Insights of Imam Mohammed allows the thinking person to venture deep into the theories or traditions and make connections that do not appear on the surface or first impression presented by religious text. For example, the Arabic is the language of the Qur'an; it is a root language that use three letters (consonants) in each word that go to the root meaning of those the three letters, it is most useful in the critical thinking process.

ALLAH says this is an Arabic Qur'an...He also says he created man's languages...No culture created language without help from Allah. The word Arabic is rooted in Rabb an attribute of Allah. The basic of the words "ARABIC" and "RABB" is "RAB." Although it is just two consonants R and B, the connection is the same. Allah says in the Qur'an the He is Rabb Alamiin—Lord (Nourisher) of the all the worlds. Nourisher of All systems of knowledge is the expression that Imam Mohammed uses for this Attribute and this statement. In essence, Al-Rabb is He who nurtures, cultivates and encourages life.

Therefore, we should understand that the Arabic language is the best language to nourish and encourage human understanding especially as it pertains to the concepts that are revealed to the human mind by the Creator.

The language allows us to make connections easily because the meaning of the word is connected to the root concept. For instance, the Arabic word Malaa ikaa means Angel in English; and the word Al-Malik. Al-Malik is one of the ninety-nine attributes of Allah; generally, it means The King, The Master, The Sovereign Lord. In the verb form Malaka, it is to own, possess, have power or dominion over, and to rule. Al-Malik and Malaaika are connected by the letters MLK.

With the English words Ruler and Angel, there are no lines of site connection... Ruler (G-d) and Angel are not spelled or look similar in letter recognition. From the beginning to the end of each word there is not a resemblance. This same problem is true with their meanings of each word. Ruler (G-d) means the Supreme Being having complete sovereignty of His Creation; Angel is a form a of a Greek word "messenger." While a connection is there, it is not strong. It does not explain other important qualities, traits or features of this very important creation. However, on the other hand, this factor is defined more comprehensive in Arabic.

After some reasoning and deep thinking, it becomes easier to make the connection that one (Al-Malik) is the Ruler or Law Giver, and the other (Malaa'ikaa) is the force that carries out or executes the order. This is the relationship that puts and keeps the Creation in motion.

The general consensus is that Allah, the Law Giver and Ruler, has control of the entire creation; therefore, the Attribute Al-Malik defines that action.

From smallest particle to the furthest star, there is nothing in this creation that can move on its own. It operates by the permission or command of Allah; even that which appears to be motionless can't exist without his permission.

Allah has Rules and Laws for everything; the force or system that executes these laws and rules Allah calls it Malaa'ika. This is from His attribute Al Maliik.

The Malaa'ika is like the Executive Branch of the United States of America's government; it executes the laws to keep order. The Malaa'ika is the invisible force that was created to make creation move or stand still. We see the effects of it, but the system is not seen by the naked eye, even the human body is part of this system.

The blood, heart, eyes and literally everything in and on the human body operate at the pleasure of Allah by way of His system, Malaa'ikaa. It operates in everything and everywhere. One of the things that the system does not force is our conscious mind; it can influence our thoughts, but not control them. Actually, this entire system (Malaa ikaa) was instructed by Allah to obey the

151

conscious mind of the human being. This point is found in the Qur'an, Suratul Baqarah, Ayah 34. "And behold, We said to the angels: "Bow down to Adam:' and they bowed down: not so Ibliis: he refused and was haughty: and he was of those who reject faith."

Allah made all Malaa'ikaa to "bow down" or make "sujudah" to the conscious mind. This meant that they were commanded to assist man by way of encouragement or relinquishing their power to man. This includes our physical body; it has to obey the mind. As you can see that the only thing that did not bow was Ibliis.

Here, Ibliis is the force that degenerated from the "Jinn" which is the emotional capacity in all living creatures. That particular emotion that Ibliis represent is haughty which is viewed as proud, arrogant, conceited or self-important. These are just several emotions in this category that are troublesome for the human being. To this concept, Allah gives the name Ibliis.

The names and images that Allah gave these and other forces were for our benefit. 1,400 years ago, at the time the Qur'an was revealed, the populace intellectual growth could not comprehend these concepts in this rational manner. Therefore, the conscious mind could understand these ideas best in a picture presentation.

Pictures make it easier for us to comprehend a scholarly idea or concept with a universal message. No matter the depth of the concept, human comprehension began in primitive behavior. We know this to be true because early in our history, our first written language was the drawing of pictures to communicate ideas.

Our form of communication was born out of picture language. In fact, written symbols are sticks, elliptical shapes and lines placed in a particular position to give meaning to them. We see pictures in our mind to help us understand abstract concepts. The picture of Allah's command to the Malaa'ikaa (the Angels) was a most significant event in our existence.

In essence, the Malaa'ikaa comes right down to Imam Mohammed's definition, "An existence that is to serve man and help man get the victory. They respond automatically but only to good."

As powerful as these concepts were, they were not the beginning of the rational approach to knowledge Imam Mohammed introduce to his followers. One the earliest he began with was the creation of Adam. He pointed out that as male and female meaning "he them" simply meant that the first community of humans was named Adam. While an individual is the lowest common denominator of community life, it is family life that is the foundation for all communities including countries and nations.

In the scripture, especially the Bible, the forming of humanity is repeated in different ways, however, it emphatically points out that family is the beginning.

Genesis verse 26 says, "And God said, Let us make man in our image, after our likeness: and let them have dominion over the fish of the sea, and over the fowl of air, and over the cattle, and over all the earth, and over every creeping thing that creepeth upon the earth." Verse 27 says, "So God created man in his own image, in the image of God created he him; male and female created he them."

These two verses are among the most misunderstood verses of the Bible. They offer a wonderful challenge for the mind to analyze and grasp. They invite the reader to use their rational mind and investigate this magnificent concept. Yet, this wonderful request is not accepted by most readers. The challenge is discovering what the concept actually reveals.

First, our image is unique to other creatures. In this passage, it stresses that the human being was created different from other creatures. We have our own unique image. Each creature has its own unique image that is true to its species—a quality that identifies its appearance, behavior and abilities from all the innumerable creatures in the universe. Like the human being, some creatures have a special characteristic. The human being's special characteristic is that we are a limited creator; one whose powers are within a certain boundary. We are creators in a minor way, in that, to create something such as a car; we must start with the physical creation. We create from the Creation. No other creature can alter, shape and develop the physical world like the human being. This is our special characteristic; our image. The Creator has created the human being with this power from Himself.

Second, The Creator created everything from nothing; this is a concept that the human being does not have the mental capacity to conceive. Our brain can't even think of nothing. To us it is just a word. Our minds cannot imagine nothing.

Therefore, the only concept that is within our mental reach is an abstract that would not qualify as the absence of everything. These are the limitations in which we are created; whereas, Allah, The Creator, has no limitations or boundaries.

This concept is also found in the Qur'an. It reflects on this idea about our creation.

It starts with Ayah 30 in Suratul Al Baqarah, and continues 31 thru 43. It describes that Allah created the Khalifah (human beings) and taught us the nature of everything by giving us the power to investigate, discover, and shape the creation. He commanded everything to assist us in that challenge.

Allah created the conscious mind with its intellect to engage the creation, an emotional component for stimulation and appreciation, and a soul (Nafs) for moral guidance. This was the fusion of mind (spiritual) with a physical body (earth)...it was an amalgamation that operates as one with the conscious mind in charge and held responsible. The evidence of this creation occurred thousands of years ago the moment when, in our early history as we ran with the pre-historic animals, we stopped and began to use our intellect to evolve ourselves out of animal life into human life.

In the Qur'an, in Arabiyyah, Allah created the human being to rule over the creation by His permission; He called us the "Khalifah; Adam is the proper name of the Khalifah. In Arabic, the word Khalifah has many meaning, each magnifying the nature of the Khalifah; Imam Mohammed pointed out that one of the main meanings of this word is, "One who thinks for himself." That meaning shows a great deal of freedom that the Creator gave to His creature, to be independent in making decisions. This idea ties to another meaning which is to "go against or oppose."

Allah created the Khalifah with the mental power to oppose Him. In fact, we do not have to believe in Allah. The choice is ours; however, that is not the reason for that power. With this power, we have demonstrated over time that we were created not to obey the natural laws, but follow our inclination that was derived from our understanding of those laws. The human being defied the law of gravity, splits the atom and achieved thousands of other feats because we were created to think for ourselves and follow that thought. We challenge the creation and in many cases disregard the natural laws that other creatures are bound by. They can't change their circumstances because of these laws. For this reason, it is not difficult to see that the name Khalifah is derived from the Attribute "Al-Khaliq" or "The Creator."

In fact, Al-Khaliq means the only One that can create from nothing. However, The Creator has given a portion of His Attribute to the Khalifah to change the world and bring another creation into existence at His leave. Still,

157

there are other interesting meanings of Khalifah such as viceroy, successor or from behind; then again, the most telling of them all is succeeding generation.

Succeeding generation is the one definition that identifies the existence of evolution. It is this idea that the Khalifah grows by each new generation improving on the advancements of the previous generation. If we had to start from scratch every generation, we would never make progress; we would be as the other creature—not evolving. This is the single factor that accounts for human evolution. A summarizing point about the Khalifah was made when Imam Mohammed said, "Man was Created to find truth and see clearly. Come by way of Creation to G-d."

The Blessings from Allah are incalculable; yet, the one that ranks right up at the top is His command to the Angels to allow the Khalifah to have complete access to the creation. This transpired in Ayah 34 as Allah commanded them to bow. The word is actually sajaduu (prostration). This Ayah is one that scholars outside of our community don't seem to understand at all. They almost entirely miss the concept. Thanks to Allah, Imam Mohammed got it, and expressed in terms we could understand.

As his insight strengthened, he defined elements and the meanings. Scripture used elements such as water to describe a concept. Case in point is in the story of Moses and the Red Sea.

Water, for example, represents our natural sentiments or human sensitivities and deep feelings. Although it is not mentioned in different Ayah, the sea is called the Red Sea. In religious language, red represents passions and uninhibited social life. Subsequently, the hypocrisy in the people, their pretense and finally betrayal, will be drowned in their hearts, and they could pass over into a new life (the new way of thinking). However, for those who could not give up these emotions, Allah will cover or overwhelm them in their own sentiments; they will lose the opportunity for growth in their spiritual life. They will remain in their material development.

When Imam Mohammed began to unravel the methodology of Fard, the Ministers and other Leaders (Chiefs of Pharaoh) in the Nation of Islam went back and forth in their decision to be with the Imam. They and their followers loved the material growth under the Nation of Islam so much that they could not cross over to spiritual life and understanding. Subsequently, they were engulfed in their passions or sentiments to stay in Fard's symbolic world.

However, for Imam Mohammed, it was full steam ahead. He taught the people seemingly nonstop. For the following years, he was traveling and speaking throughout the country, producing weekly radio broadcasts, writing newspaper articles and books. He filled the airways with his insight that was viewed as a new language that brought understanding to religious text. His insight was being saturating to the Nation of Islam; the doctor was giving birth to the child.

Imam Mohammed recognized the concept that identified a Divine pattern on which the Creator fashioned the human being; the pattern of Human Excellence.

He came to the conclusion that the Divine Word is referred to as life-giving truth; it works within as an unlocking of the mind that turns the light on in our being, and makes a spiritual sun to rise within us; it shines upon the dead matter in our mind, our soul, and our spirit. It carries the germ of Divine Mind which is an expression of the realities that is the Creator.

It became increasingly clear that the pattern of Human Excellence was the pattern that would build an excellent world. In addition, Human Excellence was supported and shaped by the Moral Conscious which comes from the natural awareness of the Creator that appeared in early man as fear of something greater than himself.

He enlighten this new community with this concept as he discussed how early man feared thunder, lightning and other natural phenomenon. As man evolved, this fear grew into respect and the vehicle that caused his search for the Creator. The Qur'an calls this process "Taqwa." It is Taqwa that assist in forming our Moral Conscious. The Moral Conscience is an expression of the soul or Nafsin in the Qur'an.

In Suratul Al Shams (The Sun), in Ayat 7-10, "By the Soul and the proportion and order given to it; And its enlightenment as to its wrong and its right; Truly he succeeds that purifies it. And he fails that corrupts it!" Transliteration "Wa nafsi wa maa saw wa haa Fa 'alhamahaa fujuu rahaa wa *taqwaa* haa   Qad aflaha man *zakaahaa* Wa qad kaaba man dasaahaa."

This concept applies to the individual as well as the society. As long as the human being consciously follows their Moral Conscience, this pattern would guide them to build a better society. The moment that the human being deviates from his Moral Conscience, they began to corrupt this pattern, and the world would reflect that corruption.

Religious text shows this swerving from the path in three symbols in the place that most religious books call the Garden. As elaborate as the story in the garden, the essence of it is simple to grasp.

The first symbol is Adam. The second is the woman called Eve. The third is the serpent or snake. It is most important to understand that these are religious symbols that identify a characteristic in the human being's makeup; they are not to be taken for an actual man, woman or serpent.

The man is the symbol for the conscious mind in the human being. The woman is symbolic to our emotions, and the serpent represents our rational mind. The story in the garden reflects the Creator instructing our conscious mind not to let our emotions or rationale lead us. He says, "Don't approach this tree." That is directed at the conscious mind, if it follows that instruction, it is a sign of following our Moral Conscience. Instead, it followed the emotions (symbolized by the woman) and rational mind (symbolized as the serpent) we fell into ruin.

However, even though we may make mistakes, the very moment the human being returns to following our Moral Conscience, the pattern of Human Excellence will re-establish correct life and a wonderful society.

The gravity of the concept lies in the term human. The idea in the Qur'an says that Allah created man on the straightway as it points out the nature of man, especially with the term Bashar. The term "Bashir," good news bringer, is rooted in the same as bashar. Allah instructs Prophet Muhammad in the Qur'an, "Say! I am a human mortal like you". Bashar means mortal, and the mortal means sensitive, a sensitive life. Imam Mohammed said, "There are some pious people, they are turned on to Muhammad the Prophet as "Bashir" so much they refer to him as "Sayyedenaa Bashar" translated "Our master," the human model."

Another term of interest is Insaan. It is used in the Qur'an to describe the human being as a thinking creature. This is in conjunction with the technical term for the human being "Homo Sapiens" which also means thinking creature.

The term sapiens is a form of sapient which is rooted in sage or sagacity. Commonly, sage is referred to as healthy; it is used as a medicinal herb and in flavoring meats. On the other hand, technically, term is from *sapere* to taste, having good taste, to be wise. Thus, sapient is defined as possessing or expressing great sagacity, wisdom or discernment.

It is important to keep in mind that thinking creature is only one part of the importance of understanding "Human;" it addresses the meaning of "man" in human. In essence, man means mind: This is one of the first things we learned from Imam Mohammed. But, man is preceded by the prefix "hu."

Hue is the proper name for "hu." While, it is mostly referred to as color, it is more about the shades, tones and quality of color. Once we grasp that color also relates to the character of man. It is the emotions of the human being. The emotion it represents most is passion. Upon examining the word passion, it is also in two parts; the first is pass; the second is sion. The suffix "sion" means in the act of. Whereas, pass means to go by, find a way around, accept, to get ahead, leave behind or even overtake. As the two are put together as in passion they mean excitement, craze, enthusiasm, zeal and hundreds of terms that define pure emotion. According to most definitions, it means intense emotion, compelling action; it applies to an emotion that is deeply stirring or ungovernable. In fact, it is unchecked emotion. Therefore, the Hue in human represents the checking of our emotions by the use of our Moral Conscience.

Our Moral Conscience is what governs and controls passion and intellect. In essence, the thinking creature's intellect is proceeded by its compassion or controlling its emotions. The human being must strive for the excellence in his character which should be driven by our compassionate nature, and the Moral Conscience directs the action toward right or civil conduct as it relates to consideration for the condition of others.

Imam Mohammed found the evidence to support the concept of Human Excellence in materials he studied, especially the Qur'an. He became a student of the Bible and Qur'an. To convey this concept, he had to develop a New Language that would unlock the secrets of ancient thinkers and interpret the picture language in the Qur'an and Bible. Also, and perhaps just as important, he had to help prepare the community to use that language as a tool for human salvation.

Preparation is very important; however, in order to benefit from it, we must recognize that we are a community (Ummah), and not an association, organization or a corporation. The Qur'an, Bible or any revelation indicated that Allah intended to bring into existence anything other than a community.

Having the language of Imam Mohammed, we must take the form of the first community established on the order of Ibrahiim (Abraham) as Allah created it. Allah has revealed to the world in the Qur'an and other scripture that He will make an Ummah; not just any Ummah, but one that is just and balanced (a unique community not given to extremes)!

Qur'an 4: 125 say, "And who can better in religion than one who submits his whole self to Allah, does good, and follows the way of Abraham the true in faith? For Allah did take Abraham for a friend." We must understand that we are a community established on the Millah of Abraham; the hopes Abraham for a better society. This will determine our destiny. Once we are past this first hurdle, we must become familiar with and be willing to fulfill our mission for which we have been prepared. We need to be clear on who and what we are. To acquaint ourselves with this, perhaps, it is best that we examine the properties of the words association, organization, corporation and community. This should assist us in determining which of them fits the term Ummah that Allah uses in the Qur'an; and, the concept of community life expressed by Imam Mohammed.

While examining these terms, it is of the utmost importance to view as a means to an end, not as to condemn any or all of them. We must see all of them as having good and useful qualities in one form or another.

One of the points that Imam Mohammed made often was "words make people." With this in mind, what we are looking for is what Allah has pointed out to us in the life of His Prophets and by way of Revelations. The concept must support life. Using a sober rational approach, we must bring a concept to a logical conclusion by following the line of logic.

LIFE as defined by Imam Mohammed is something that exists in some kind of environment that supports it. The key factor is the continuation of an entity (a body, thing or creature). And, that continuation is supported by its surroundings. The Imam added that, "a continuous evolutionary progression from inorganic to human development." Thus, we are looking for what supports life...a total life. "We are to be conscious of that life and have respect for that life and build on that life, so that it will grow and become more useful for ourselves and more useful for mankind," said Imam Mohammed.

Prophet Abraham represents community life; he turned from individual concerns to focus on group interest. Community concerns improve the living conditions of a society and move it forward.

Community (Ummah) is more than just people or humanity. It is the ultimate social grouping of humanity. It is when people come together on common grounds for common ideas or goals. In essence, it is people having, working and striving for common interest.

People that live in the same neighborhood are referred to as a community because the same things affect them. They work to improve on that life they have in common. On the other hand, the place where people live may not define their community. It comes into existence and stays alive because of its beliefs and behaviors of the members, and yet they may not live in the same neighborhood. Regardless of how or why a community exists, the sky is the limit as to what it stands for or the tactics it uses to promote its ideology. It could be a Mafia, Jim Jones or Society to save the Whales. The extremes don't define the community; it's the common interest of the people.

The community life that Allah intends for the human beings is a balanced one. A community life that is not too far to the left or to the right, one that is in the middle that everyone could gravitate to. It is neither so materially focused that it loses its spirituality (Moral Conscience) nor is it so spiritual that it is not fixed in the reality of the physical life.

In the ascent of Prophet Muhammed, the last stage was the station or level of Abraham. This signaled the beginning of the community life that Prophet

Muhammed built in Medina. That humble beginning ushered in the advances in the 20th century.

His powerful example serves as a blueprint for our future. How he related to other people as well as those in his immediate community was one of working together for the common good or concerns of all the people. He even established that one should deal with an enemy with humility. The Qur'an is the guide for social behavior that he used to achieve this balanced community.

Spirit of Bilal

CHAPTER 16

STRUCTURING THE COMMUNITY

Simultaneous to bringing the community into Al-Islam proper and establishing a new Insight (Tafsir) in religion, Imam Mohammed had to deal with the organizational structure as well as its philosophy. The structure of the Nation of Islam was that of an organization and not that of a community. Although there many facets that resembled community life, it was a very strict Autocracy where all power and authority is held by a single, self-appointed individual; generally, that individual is a charismatic leader. In the case of the Nation of Islam, it started with Fard, and he passed his authority to the Honorable Elijah Muhammad. This authority was passed to Imam Mohammed by the ministers and officials of the Nation after the passing of the Honorable Elijah Muhammad. Although this is not in keeping with the concept of the structure of the community in the Qur'an, in some cases, it is beneficial to the group.

Case in point, the Honorable Elijah Muhammad reigned for 40 years. During which time, history shows that he had accomplished great achievements for the African-American people while elevating their standard of life. Contrarily, in an autocracy position, leaders such as Jim

Jones and Adolph Hitler were the damnation of their followers and people.

Jim Jones caused the death of hundreds of his unquestioning followers by convincing them that death was better than life in this world. He got them to commit mass suicide by drinking a poison in the form of Kool-Aid...this included men, women and children. Just as dangerous, but differently, Hitler slaughter thousands of innocent Jews during World War II by death squads, gas chambers and the kill at will attitude of his soldiers. Both Jones and Hitler are prime examples of the abuse of authority in its worst form. In other words, as it has often been stated, "Power corrupts and absolute power corrupts absolutely."

The contrast between them and The Honorable Elijah Muhammad demonstrates that the autocracy form of leadership can go from one extreme to another depending on the personality and disposition of its leader. It is very difficult for a potential follower to initially judge whether the person that they will align with is a psychopath or not...this is the underlying principle that put the followers at risk. A very good explanation of this type of situation and authority is in Imam Mohammed's use of the Arabic term Bashar.

Bashar, one who is alive to the needs of his fellow man...alive to the life of his fellow man as he is alive to his own life. "And really he becomes more alive to his own life when he becomes more humanly sensitive. So this is the "Sayyedenaa Bashar," The humanly sensitive person," the Imam stated.

"When the leaders," he continued, "who do not have the "Bashar" development they are not humanly sensitive, when they get into authority and they start ordering the society and influencing the order of the society they can take us into an ugly and hard, oppressive society and it will punish us rather than show us mercy. It will give us pain and misery rather than mercy or compassion."

This is the most important reason that this secular structure is among the least favored, and cannot work or preserve the nature or integrity of community life. The Imam also stated that closest form of leadership or government in the secular world to Al-Islam was a democracy. While it has its shortcomings; it is for the people by the people in theory.

However, the community that Allah established to cultivate the garden has as its head the Word of Allah. This does not conflict with the secular world (the tree in mist of the garden) it actually is a benefit to it. But, it is

173

a community that cannot be compromised or it loses its innocence. Therefore, it does not matter what kind of secular structure that was in place when Imam Mohammed came into the Leadership role, the fact of the matter is that it had to be done away with, and replaced with a community life. From this point, those who wanted to support his leadership had to make the commitment to follow his concept of a community.

While deciphering Fard's language, he began to dismantle the structure by telling the members, now his followers, that "We are not a Nation. We are a Community. America is a nation, and a great nation. We are a community in that nation." He renamed the organization "The World Community of Islam in the West (WCIW). This signaled the many changes to come over the following years. He changed his title from Supreme Minister to Imam in conjunction with changing the title of all the Ministers to Imam. This was followed by changing the names of Muhammad Mosques and Temples to Masjid. The followers began legally shedding their Christian names and giving themselves Arabic names from the Holy Qur'an.

He eliminated its chain of command structure by abolishing local and national positions of Captain, Lieutenant, Inspector, Fruit of Islam (FOI) and Muslim

Girl Training (MGT). This left each Masjid and Islamic Center with an Imam of their choice as their representative. Each Masjid or Center would establish mutual consultation (a committee of its members to govern its affairs). In other words, each Masjid or Islamic Center was autonomous; they were independent and free of national or regional authority or control.

He took the national newspaper, the Muhammad Speaks, and changed its name in the following order: Bilalian News, World Muslim News, A.M. Journal, and Muslim Journal. He turned it over into a corporation owned by stockholders and managed by a Board of Directors.

Conditioning the thinking of his followers, he changed the name of the organization from "World Community of Islam in the West" to the "American Muslim Mission." Soon afterwards, he modified the name for the organization. After adapting a new name "The Muslim American Society," the community found itself in a legal struggle for the name and trademark (MAS) with an emigrant group that had the same name. After contemplating, the Imam decided to change to the organization's final name, "American Society of Muslim." He also made the comment that "we really

175

don't need a name." This was the final name of the organization, but not the final action of Imam Mohammed.

August 30, 2003, Imam Mohammed resigned as leader of the American Society of Muslim. This was the last step in dismantling the secular structure of the original Nation of Islam. The followers were left with two choices; to go back to the old organizational structure or become a community practicing full autonomy. The organizational structure established by Muhammad Abdullah (Master Fard) and passed down from the Honorable Elijah Muhammad to Imam Mohammed was finished...it was time for the followers to sink or swim in the lake of reality; we had to shed the secular structures and grow and develop a community life.

There were some who tried to dig up the bones and return to the old organizational structure. They responded like the slave on the plantation who did not know how to react to their freedom; they did not want to leave the master's house. On the other hand, many began to accept the concept of autonomy that forms the makeup of community life that Allah reflects in the Qur'an. For the next five years, the community strengthened in its understanding and acceptance of the new life...no boss, leader or illah except Allah. Imam Mohammed was preparing us for the inevitable!

The inevitable took place September 9, 2008. Imam Mohammed passed his community life into the people. We became him in spirit...we are the community who's common interest in the in insight (Tafsir) of Imam Mohammed. Allah's Ruh (Spirit) that He breathed into the African-American people took root in the Nation of Islam and matured in the language of Imam W. D. Mohammed; this bonded us as a community with one Lord, Allah.

We are unique! Not in the sense of better or worse than other people, just in the sense of having a characteristic that set us aside as other people that have their unique identity also. They are different in some way, existing as the only one or as the sole example; single; solitary in type or characteristics. Ethnic groups have their uniqueness. Nearly all creatures, cultures, society, communities and nationalities are identified by their uniqueness. We are identified by the Language of Imam Mohammed; this gave us our own Madh'hab (school of thought).

It was Allah who made us unique. He says in the Qur'an that he made all of us different so we can learn from one another (know each other). He created us as a

177

community to resurrect the spirit of the original community established by Prophet Muhammed 1400 years ago. To accomplish this task, we must bring religious solidarity, harmony and a social order to the general society with a new language that Allah blessed Imam Mohammed with.

Much like a culture, an Ummah can pass from one generation to the next and maintain its integrity. As each generation is born, it learns and lives according to the common interest of the parents, and these subtleties become a way of life for them...they can do this without any documentation or orders. More important, almost anyone can become a part by simply accepting the common interest whenever possible. The concept of an Ummah may be much bigger than some of the English labels that we may give it. However, we should still explore some of these labels for our own reasoning; keeping in mind that none of them may truly define Ummah.

While we cannot look out of Imam Mohammed's eyes to see his vision of us as a community, we can certainly use his process to utilize rational thinking to follow a connection to its logical conclusion. Foremost, what makes us a community is a far deeper connection than that of any organization or other social groups

Whereas, Ummah and community are words that in their natural forms are nouns. While it is true that community originates from two words combined, it is still in the noun form. The two nouns that make it up are "common" and "unity." Common means belonging to or shared by two or more individuals, and unity is a definite amount being made one. Therefore, based on this simple breakdown, it is clear that of the four words: association, organization, corporation and community, the closet to the Qur'anic term "Ummah" is Community.

The community life that Allah intends for the human beings is a balanced one. A community life that is not to far to the left or to the right, one that is in the middle that everyone could gravitate to. It is neither so materially focused that it loses its spirituality (Moral Conscience) nor is it so spiritual that it is not fixed in the reality of the physical life. This emphasized in the story of Prophet Ibrahiim and the life of Prophet Muhammed, May the Peace and Blessings of Allah be on them both.

In Surah Al Hujuraat 49:13 Allah says, "O mankind! We created you from a single (pair) of a male and a female, and made you into Nations and tribes, that ye may know each other…" While very important, the terms nations and tribes are different from one another as well as from a community (Ummah). Firstly, in this instance, neither nations nor tribes are rooted in the Arabic word Ummah. Secondly, nations is a political term that refers to a state, country, land, homeland or inhabitants; Tribe is a term that classifies social groupings through blood lines such as in clans, family unit or tree, ancestors, ethnic group and lineage; whereas, the characteristic of a community is "common interest."

Not to subordinate the importance of nations and tribes, alternatively, the social group that community is frequently confused with is an organization. This is because like community an organization is connected by purpose or task which is sometimes thought of as common interest. However, once we learn the origin of words and why they are used, it becomes an easier chore to make a distinction.

Basically, once a community takes on another social groups form, it reverses its community category. It becomes a social group that resembles or functions as one of the other social groups mentioned.

By its nature, a community does not require or need a leader because they, a group of peers that already have a center, common interest or focal point. This is the reason Allah chose Ummah, because it can operate at his direction, and not have an intercessor. His community would not have to function under different personalities. It would not run the risk of having a brilliant or poor leader. Everyone would be free to follow the word according to their understanding. It does not require a head other then the word of Allah. In reality, Allah is its head.

Nearly all of us, live in a community we call a residential community...there are no leaders. However, within most communities, there are organizations that perform tasks, assignments, duties, undertakings, and administrative activities. They can range from Block Associations, Boy or Girl Scouts to the Federal Government. To get a particular task done it is better have an organization for that specific task. Once in his public lecture, Imam Warith Deen Mohammed mentioned, "we need organization as much as we need religion." In the language of Imam Mohammed and the Qur'an, Prophet Abraham represents community life; he turned from individual concerns to focus on group interests. Community concerns improve the living conditions of a society and move it forward.

Spirit of Bilal

CHAPTER 17

RAISING A WITNESS

It is written in the Qur'an that Allah points out that every community will have a Witness (standard) from amongst their own people. This person is the Standard by which the people are measured in terms of their conduct conforming to the message that was giving to Prophet Muhammed. The Standard by which everyone's moral conduct is measured is the life example of Prophet Muhammad.

Each witness will serve as proof within his generation that the Qur'an and life example of Muhammad raised him. This process eliminates any excuse that people can have about a clear understanding of the message, because it will be explained to them by one who has the same origin: common experience, ancestry, interest and sensitivities.

It becomes easy to understand the plan that Allah had in place once all the pieces are put together. Another fact is necessary to complete the picture of Imam Mohammed. Concurrent with his work of restructuring the Nation of Islam and developing a common interest that bonded the group into a new community, he was raised by Allah for an additional purpose—to be one to continue the call to humanity for them to raise their conscience to achieve human excellence.

The evidence of that reality is highlighted in Suurah Al Nahl (The Bees) in Ayah 84 & 89 of the Qur'an. However, perhaps it is best to first examine the concept of the Surah in which these Ayah appear.

The Bees, as the Surah is named, is the 16th Suurah in the Qur'an. It is named after Ayyat 68-69 where in Allah tells us of the bee and its value. Of them He says, "And thy Lord taught the Bee to build its cells in hills on trees and in (men's) habitations;" This indicate that they coexist near humans' living environment. The next verse says, "Then to eat of all the produce (of the earth) and find with skill the spacious paths of its Lord: there issues from within their bodies a drink of varying colors wherein is healing for men: verily in this is a Sign for those who give thought." Scholars agree that the drink is honey, and most scientists agree that it does have healing purposes.

There is another fascinating aspect about the Bee. The Honey Bees, as pointed out, are generalist floral visitors, and will pollinate a large variety of plants...they assist in the fertilization of plant life as they visit plant after plant collecting and depositing pollen at each plant in preparation to produce their nectar (honey).

Man has been utilizing the value of honey and learning a lesson from its producer. A community of honey bees has often been employed throughout history by political theorists as a model of human society. For us, it is much more; Allah says it is a sign. It is centered on the dual action of their nature. First, the honey they produce serves as a tasteful healing food for the human being. Second, in the pollination process, they use other life forms to reproduce implies service to other forms of life than their own.

These are two aspects that convey the message of spiritual healing for human guidance. We find that it is most beautiful that Allah gives clear evidence of His Mercy for humanity by raising in each community a witness as pointed out in Surah Al Nahl (The Bees). To achieve ease of understanding of the following Ayyat (84 and 89), they are presented in the Arabic and English.

Ayyah 84

185

Ali: "One day We shall raise from all peoples a witness: then will no excuse be accepted from Unbelievers nor will they receive any favors."

Pickthall: "And (bethink you of) the day when We raise up of every nation a witness, then there is no leave for disbelievers, nor are they allowed to make amends."

Ayat 89

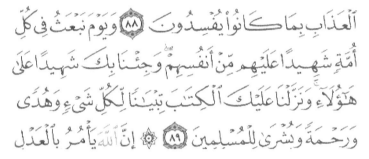

Ali: "One day We shall raise from all peoples a witness against them from amongst themselves: and We shall bring thee as a witness against these (thy people): and We have sent down to thee the Book explaining all things a guide, a Mercy and glad tidings to Muslims."

Pickthall: "And (bethink you of) the day when We raise in every nation a witness against them of their own folk, and We bring thee (Muhammad) as a witness against these. And We reveal the Scripture unto thee as an exposition of all things, and a guidance and a mercy and good tidings for those who have surrendered (to Allah)."

Wa yauma nab'asu fi kulli ummatin shahidan 'alaihim min anfusihim wa ji'na_ bika shahidan 'ala_ ha_'ula_'(i), wa nazzalna_ 'alaikal kita_ba tibya_nal likulli syai'iw wa hudaw wa rahmataw wa busyra_ lil muslimin(a).

These Ayah are very clear in the Arabiyyah, but it is necessary to examine both English translations, and compare them to the Arabic text. For instance, Yusuf Ali uses peoples, and Pickthall uses nation for the Arabic word Ummatin (plural for Ummah). Community is the best term to use because it identifies a particular or mutual characteristic or common interest of a group. Also, it can be applicable to other creations; whereas, neither peoples nor nation are interchangeable with creatures such as Bees, Birds, Wolves and a host of other creatures. Allah makes it plain in Surah Al An 'aam 6:38 as He says, "There is not an animal (that lives) on the earth nor a being that flies on its wings but (forms part of) communities like you." In this Ayyat, the Arabic word for communities is umamun. This is the same root as Ummatan. As a consequence, of the English words: peoples, nation and communities, it is clear that community is the correct word for the Arabic "ummatin."

Before we can proceed with how these Ayat should read in English, there are two other minor words that must be mentioned. They are the Arabic "min" for the English word "from" or "of," and "fi" for the English "in." These two words are not really interchangeable. Pickthall uses the word "in" for the word "fi." However, Yusuf Ali never uses the English word "from" for the Arabic "fi" in his translation. On the other hand, Pickthall uses the word "of" for the Arabic word "min;" whereas, Yusuf Ali uses "from" for the same word.

The Arabic word "fi" appears in the second ayah just before the word "kulli." By the way, Kulli means each and every one or all.

These verses become crystal clear when these suggestions are made. Another point is the word Shaheedan for witness. Both translators use witness rather than the word witnesses because it is still in the singular form; although it is talking about many communities, it means one witness per community. It may be just an oversight in the transliteration because the Arabic is shaheedan not shahidan; One is witness and the other is martyr.

Lastly, in ayah 89, the phrase "from amongst themselves" is strong, but it not as strong as the actual Arabic "anfusihim." This word comes from "nafs" the soul. It is also translated to mean of the same spirit, mind; life; psyche; and the same yolk or experience. In substance, this understanding is much stronger. It integrates the social, physical and spiritual life of the community. This addresses the fact that the person must be indigenous (born in the same condition and circumstance).

This concluding point in the last statement is different than from Yusuf Ali or Pickthall because they both imply that the Prophet is going to witness against the Ummah or community. Whereas, in the first part of the ayah, it says that the witness from them will witness against them. This indicates that the Prophet or his life example is checking the witnesses when is says "these". By using the word "these" it is showing that there are many witnesses, but one per community. All of this may seem like small bones or points, but they can make a big difference in what we think and understand.

To that point, while there are several ways to paraphrase the English of these two Ayah, the following is offered as only one:

84. There is coming a day for every community when We will raise a witness from among them: then no excuses will be accepted from the Unbelievers nor are they allowed to make atonement.

89. There is coming a day for every community when We will raise in them a witness against them from their own spirit, background and experience: We shall bring thee (Muhammed's life example is the litmus test) as a witness against these witnesses who were raised up.

Regardless of how these Ayat are paraphrased, history will prove that there has not been an indigenous person born in America with the depth of understanding from an unique American point of view of the Qur'an and the life example of Prophet Muhammed as did Imam Warith Deen Mohammed. It is he who can be Shahidullah or the Witness of Allah. As an African-American, his occurrence is consistent with the Qur'an. Furthermore, his body of knowledge (Tafsir) is unequalled in this modern era as his explanation of Al-Islam has brought clarity of religious truths to millions of Americans and especially the African-American community. He accredits his understanding solely to Allah. In fact, there is no evidence that anyone taught him his understanding. He declared that his Insight was not given to him by any human being. His interpretation of the Qur'an and Holy Bible came as a result of his sincerity, having an open mind and the guidance of Allah. For example, one excellent illustration of his understanding is in his explanation of the concept honey as a healing for the human being was taken to another level in his Tafsir.

In a lecture in 1978, he gave the practical meaning of the symbols of milk and honey. He used the scripture that depicted the Exodus of the Hebrews from Egypt. He said, "The milk comes from spiritual disciplines, be kind, be clean, appreciate your parents, the first fruits of the breast, made for the baby." This is an explanation to show that courtesy and decency is the beginning of human life. He continued in his interpretation in these words, "But the manna is the honey, as each bee makes his honey for his own hole, or his own house, and that's what we are to do with the knowledge. Don't leave it out, take the knowledge into your own consciousness and you will get the benefit. Smelling it is nice but the greatest satisfaction comes from applying it." Here he emphasizes that it is not enough to stand on the sideline and talk. We must be an active part in competing and building a better society.

Imam Warith Deen Mohammed is the witness; where is the proof that the transformed Nation of Islam inherited by Imam Mohammed which was born out of the African-American people is that community (Ummah)? More important, is it the community that Allah will transform and raise to call the world to Human Excellence? The history of the African-American should be enough proof to support the view that they are a community fashioned like Mary in scripture.

To find the answers to these powerful questions, we must examine the history of how Imam Mohammed re-shaped the Nation of Islam into a community for humanity and not a nationalist movement. The sweet honey for the healing is the scriptures.

Allah gave us his promise and commitment in the Qur'an when He said He will raise in each and every Ummah (community) a witness of their own from themselves. This alone should satisfy us and the world. However, as an endorsement, let us inspect the facts beginning with this question, what is a community?

Suratul Al Rum 30:22

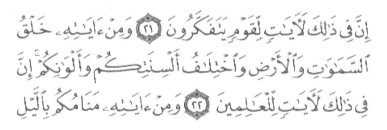

HQ Al Rum 30:22 "And among His Signs is the creation of the heavens and the earth and the variations in your languages and your colors: verily in that are Signs for those who know."   Abdullah Yusuf Ali (Translation)

"And of His signs is the creation of the heavens and the earth, and the difference of your languages and colors. Lo! herein indeed are portents for men of knowledge." Mohammad M. Pickthall (Translation)

The Holy Qur'an establishes the fact that it is Allah that created the heavens, earth and the difference in our languages and race category as well as the subtle difference within each race. But, these facts are only signs.

One of the major differences between Yusuf Ali and Pickthall is in the English translation. For example, in this Ayah, the Arabic word Ayah is used twice. Both times, Yusuf Ali translates it as "Signs." But, Pickthall in the second Ayah uses the English word "portents." Considering that portents means something that foreshadows a coming event; it is a prophetic indication or significance, Ayah must be thought of as something inevitable as well as advice on conduct. Every verse in the Qur'an is an Ayah. And in many of them Ayah is used to point out something specific. For that reason, the focus should be on intent, goal or objective as well as the literal statement or phase. Therefore, the fundamental understanding of this Ayah deals with the foundation on which something is developed, and the importance of it.

ALLAH says He created our languages. He is "Rabbil-Aalamiin." He is The Lord of All the worlds— All systems of knowledge.

All systems have a language as its foundation. Sometimes the importance of language is unnoticed even ignored as the basis for civilizations.

Language is the basic method of communicating thoughts, ideas, information and concepts. It occurs in many forms; sign, verbal, mathematical, written symbols, pictures and expressions...it is the systematic correlation of these forms that produces what we call language. It is the underpinning that societies, cultures and all forms of social groups use to start, maintain and propagate their way of life. Communication is essential to communal life. Shared life depends on communication; language is the tool. Through it, common interest is expressed as in a community. In essence, human progress is made because of language.

In the Qur'an, Allah uses picture language in similitudes to communicate concepts to us.

Surah 18 Al Kahf (The Cave) Ayat 54

"We have explained in detail in this Qur'an for the benefit of mankind every kind of similitude: but man is in most things contentious."

The word "(sad) arrafnaa" is to turn about, to display, explain, ordering, change, in other words, showing every angle. This is followed by the word "mathalin" which is a copy, resemble or to assimilate; of course, when the word "akathara" (which means to multiply) follows it, this says that these words work together to produce a prototype to assist us in recognizing very important situations in our lives.

Actually, similitude is used in the English translation to indicate a person or thing resembling another. Once recognized, we can see how Allah gives us a picture of a situation in the Qur'an that can be of use to us in our lives because it's a similar circumstance. Similar circumstance does not mean exact, it means close enough to qualify for a beneficial example.

195

Signs, on the other hand, point to an event. Yet, like similitudes, they are language based. Therefore, the language of the Qur'an is designed to cause us to think and reason. It is a guide for us to use to prepare ourselves for the future while living in the present. As a community, our place in life has been described as a coming event that has arrived. The Qur'an says, "We breathed into her of Our Spirit and We made her and her son a Sign for all peoples." This Ayah is about Maryum (Mary) and Isa (Jesus), it is prophetic. It is a sign of what Allah will do.

This is a sign of the birth of our community, and the Spirit of Allah produced a new and most important language for us by way of Imam Mohammed. This Language would prove to be the light of understanding for humanity. Imam Mohammed was an excellent servant for Allah as a witness to complete his miracle.

The Language of Imam Mohammed does not disturb the integrity of the stories loved by the Jewish, Christian and Muslim worshipers; it opens up the rational mind to see the complete concept without upsetting its basic design. Just as many other scholars of all faiths, Imam Mohammed's insight is consistent with the idea that many of the personalities in scriptures may not just address individuals, but they may speak to an all-encompassing purpose in the Creator's plan. This type of thinking suggests that the individuals represent a characteristic or conduct.

For example, a virgin is pure may represent a people who never begotten a prophet according to the Old Testament. Therefore, this implies that Mary is the symbol for that good, righteous-minded, good living, G-d fearing society type that is waiting on a prophet to be born among them. Jesus represents the Living Word of the Creator in the world. He is a society or community that is a body of spiritual knowledge, wisdom, and understanding that stands on a foundation of purity and innocence. It is a righteous community with a pure heart that has love and compassion for the suffering and rejected as did Jesus in the scripture. He is a flesh and blood community of people that live as one body or a community with one head or philosophy. The return of Jesus is not his person but it is the presence or manifestation of that one he reached of, the one his life was a sign of, the community with his spirit. This is the spirit that the Creator wills for the general society. However, in order to be exposed to the greater society, the idea must first begin a smaller community that will carry the concept of a balanced, productive and beautiful world to the greater society. With this concept in mind, we can see that both Mary and Jesus may represent communities, one giving birth to the other.

As with many signs, a real community had to be formed as the first order in this process. A virgin community had to be made in order for the Word of the Creator to impregnate it so that a second community (the Word) could be born out of it; a community that can be viewed in history or the present. It is this reality that seals the Prophecy of the Qur'an of the Witness of Allah in America. An indigenous Muslim who was born of the same soul or spirit of those he must witness against.

For him and the world, the receipt of this concept was truly an Immaculate Conception, at the very least, a Miraculous Conception; especially, considering that the terms Immaculate, Miraculous and Conception represent most excellently this amazing experience of Imam Mohammed.

CHAPTER 18

FOCUSING

Over the choppy ocean of time, filled with many difficult and complex experiences, a new community was born to bring a clear and life given message to humanity. This enormous task began hundreds of years ago on the coast of Africa and ended as a successful delivery on September 9, 2008. On that day, the community came alive to breathe the fresh air—wisdom that would reform the world; it was the wisdom passed to it by the one that Allah raised as his Witness, Imam W. D. Mohammed.

Practically, to establish our community, we need only to follow the directions that Allah has given us, and the life example of Prophet Muhammed (PBUH). First, in the five pillars or principles in Al-Islam, Allah has given us a perfect design. Second, we need only to apply them practically for the best results. These principles are easily understood and the foundation of our religion. They are as follows:

- ❖ To testify that no deity except Allah, and Muhammed is His Messenger.

- ❖ To offer the prayers dutifully and perfectly.

- ❖ To pay Zakat (i.e. obligatory charity).

- ❖ To observe fast during the month of Ramadan.

- ❖ To perform Hajj (i.e. Pilgrimage to Mecca).

"And Islam is built upon five not six, not three, but five," stated Imam Mohammed. This is a very important fact that we must consider as foundation of our Community.

With these principles in our hearts and behavior, we must focus on what else Allah has illustrated to us in the five pillars. We may not be aware of the fact that most cultures, societies, nations, communities or any social group base their organizational structure on the very concept illustrated in these principles.

For example, the first or core principle is the Belief in Allah, and Muhammed is His messenger. This is the basic idea that all the other principles are formed around. Without it there is no reason for coming together or bringing people together into a structured group. The formation of any group begins with its philosophy or principle of its ideology.

Communism gives ownership and control of wealth and property to the state. In contrast, a Free-market is an economic system in which businesses operate without government control in matters such as pricing and wage levels. Whereas, Socialism is a political theory or system in which the means of production and distribution are controlled by the people and operated according to equity and fairness rather than market. On the other hand, a Democracy is the free and equal right of every person to participate in a system of government, often practiced by electing representatives of the people by the majority of the people. While all of these examples are clearly different descriptions and meanings, it is that definition that serves as the fundamental principle on which every aspect of each of them is built.

The next step in establishment of the group is to surround the core philosophy with what the four main categories. Depending on the formation of the group, each category is defined accordingly. First, there would the management or control of group by a governing body. Second, there would be a managing of funds and resources to avoid extravagant expenditure or waste; and, a method of obtaining funds. Third, there must be an educational process of educating people in a community or society. Forth, there is a religious or motto or saying that expresses a rule to live by. In short, these categories would be government, economy, education and religion all of which are defined in the culture of the group. The success and longevity of any group and its philosophy depends on the establishment of these principles. However, we must keep in mind that the order and importance of each category depends upon the needs or direction of the group (culture).

Because we have been blessed with the five principles of Al-Islam, the application of this thinking should come natural to us. We live them daily and Allah has place in our sub-conscience to use when it becomes necessary.

The five principles of Al-Islam make us an Islamic Community; for us, it does not stop there, we had an additional task. We must view Al-Islam as the broad picture and our community as a minor portion in that picture with a specific assignment. Our mission is simply to bring the message of human excellence to the world. However, we must be organized to achieve our mission. Our makeup has to be in accord to Allah's plan. To the by-stander observing from the sideline, we may not have the structure they view as important, but for the purpose for which Allah brought us into existence, it will be perfect.

FIRST PRIORITY: CORE PHILOSOPHY

While we were coming into existence, Allah established our first priority: The Tafsir; Understanding and Wisdom of Imam Mohammed. This serves as our common or core interest. It bonds us as a community. This is only the beginning of the rest of establishing community life is on our shoulders. Some of this has been started, however, the remaining formation is up to us; with the help of Allah, we will be successful.

This could not be made any clearer than how Imam Mohammed stated it as he said, "With G-d's Help, we can take our own interests into our own hands and make a good life for ourselves, individually and collectively. And collectively is more important than individually. Whatever we plan for ourselves individually without respecting the social community, will fail."

He continued that point as he stated, "You will not live to have it passed on to your children. It will go away with you; it will be lost with you. But if you work, not just for yourself but for the social community, then what you invest will live. That is why G-d tells us that we are one family - all people are one family, from one ancestry."

He emphasized the importance of bonding as he concluded, "He (G-d) tells us that so that we will have a sense of bond. I am bonded to others. I'm connected to others".

Certainly, we are bonded to all human beings; more specifically, we are bonded to all Muslims in Al-Islam;

but, most especially, we are bonded as a new community that Allah fused with the wisdom of Imam Mohammed. Unquestionably, this is the prime or core priority that centers our community life.

Allah has entrusted us with a defining moment in history. For that reason, in this order, we should put as a priority in our life the weekly, if not daily, study of the Qur'an, life example of Prophet Muhammad and the writings and lectures of Imam W Deen Mohammed.

Each of us should concentrate a great deal of our time on independent study and gather all the information where ever and whenever we can. We are a community in which everyone is expected to become knowledgeable enough to function autonomously if necessary.

We should consistently watch his DVD's while at home, and listen to his CD's in our vehicles in our travels. We must encourage our children and grandchildren to do the same. Additionally, to obtain value his insightful information, we should visit the local Masajid, Islamic Centers or seek online resources for this valued wisdom of Imam Mohammed. Most likely, many of us are already doing this to strengthen our spirit and broaden the scope of our knowledge; many of us understand the importance of what Allah has entrusted us with.

Having the core in place and following the pattern that Allah has established for us in the five principles, we must turn our attention to the next standard to develop a wholesome and healthy community life.

He, with the help of Allah, made us into a community respected by the world. He founded us on a common interest—his understanding or Tafsir. This wisdom makes our community unique! It gives us the power to interpret religious language, and crack open the secrets that were used to keep the world in darkness (false thinking) and weak. It bonds us together; it is single unique aspect that we have in common as a community. In it, we move as one, philosophically speaking. In addition, he put us on a path to serve Allah with a purpose. Today, it is our turn to call the world to Life. This is our first priority as a community.

It is very similar to ascension of Prophet Muhammed (PBUH). In the ascension of Prophet Muhammed (PBUH), the last stage was the station or level of Abraham. This signaled the beginning of the community life that Prophet Muhammed (PBUH) built in Medina was a sign for the world, according to Imam Mohammed. That humble beginning ushered in the advances in 20th century.

Al-Masjid an-Nabawi or the Prophet's Mosque is a great mosque in Medina, Saudi Arabia. It stands on the site of a mosque built by the Prophet Muhammad himself next to his house. Today, it is the second holiest masjid in the world after al-Haram in Mecca.

He built the original masjid after his Hijrah (emigration) to Medina in 622 AD. It was an open-air building allowing people to pass through freely with a raised platform for the reading of the Qur'an. It comprised of palm trunks and mud walls and accessed through three doors: Bab Rahmah (Door of Mercy) to the south, Bab Jibril (Door of Gabriel) to the west and Bab al-Nisa' (Door of the Women) to the east.

Inside, since there was no roof, the Prophet created a shaded area to the south of masjid called the suffrah and aligned the prayer space. Originally, the space faced north toward Jerusalem, when the qibla (prayer direction) was changed to Mecca, the prayer direction was re-oriented to the south.

The masjid served as a community center, a court, and a religious school. This was basis and foundation of community life in the Ummah. For us, this is a wonderful sign.

Spirit of Bilal

At this time in our history as we merge on the world scene as a new community, these events relate directly with us in America. In a manner of speaking, we too had ascension.

We, in our ascension, travelled through time beginning with the slave ships to the mother ship. Like the Prophet in each stage of our journey we experienced situation and events. On one hand, we faced the lashes of the slave masters whip. On the other, we were freed from white supremacy to embrace black supremacy. Finally, in our last stage, we received the gift from Allah, the Tafsir of Imam W. D. Mohammed.

We received all that we needed in the way of understanding for a new community; we must bring this wisdom to the common man (sober mind) and build a community life; America is our Medina.

Our Medina (America) is a country that practices many freedoms that are relevant to us as natural born citizens. We have the Constitution on our side and every state in these United State practices freedom of religion. Al-Islam is recognized in this country and we have a good relationship here. This is our country and we have access to all the rights provided by it.

SECOND PRIORITY: BUSINESS

Case in point, Imam Mohammed pointed out that Prophet Muhammed's (PBUH) priority was education because his people were lacking in education, and education was a path to excellence. We are reminded of this when the Prophet established the first Masjid it was also used as a school. The depth of this issue with the Prophet was pointed out in The Hadith as it related that the Prophet would free a captive if he taught one of the Prophets followers to read. There was no question that education of his people was a top priority.

Following the example set by the Prophet, Imam Mohammed stressed the importance of establishing our priorities and which of them should be attended to first. Without diminishing the importance of education, Imam Mohammed emphasized that we must develop our economy within our community.

In his book "Islam's Climate for Business Success," Imam Mohammed directs our attention to the Qur'an as Allah says, "And seek with whatever means He has availed you the Home of the Destiny, but do not forget your share of this world." The Imam encourages us to get our share of our neighborhood, city, state, America and the world.

He said that Al-Islam is a comprehensive religion that focuses on every aspect of our life. He says, "Al-Islam, is respecting and giving recognition to business in a classic way." He continues his point as he states, "The Qur'an, itself, promotes good business sense." The Imam summarized his impression on business by informing us that our community needs businesses as much as the Prophet's followers needed education. Without a strong business life in our community we will not be able to sustain community life. Our priority must be business.

Allah has given us a wonderful opportunity to call the world to human excellence, but we must establish community life. To be successful in developing business sense and momentum, we must be focused. "The disciplines that we are given in Islam for our own life are the disciplines that we need for success," Imam Mohammed said in his book "Islam's Climate for Business Success."

We can achieve this enormous task by concentrating on the existing Muslim businesses that are outwardly supporters of the Tafsir or wisdom of Imam Mohammed. Not in a casual way, but energetically and especially with our money.

We must visualize their businesses as budding endeavors, and it is our dollars that cause them to flourish into a million-dollar industry. This will help to supply jobs and economic support for the future for our community.

They are our brothers and sisters of the same experience. When we buy their goods and services, we are doing what Allah have all people to do; help themselves by doing for self. It is time for us to raise like a phoenix from ashes of our memories the "Do for Self" attitude. We must see and build industries the same way as the rest of the world.

Our businesses must build a reputation by selling excellent products and services; our prices must be competitive. We must have what our customers need or want, and get it in a timely manner. We must keep in mind the fact that people love to come into a clean looking and smelling establishment with excellent service; the customer is always right is a very good approach to success in business.

Those of us that have large or small successful businesses should think of ways to improve and grow. Some of those methods could improve the community. We should consider franchising or duplicating our business throughout the country. Additionally, we should join and form business committees; these committees of like minds can facilitate business progress. This would help others to achieve some success and make us stronger economically as a total community.

We must trust in our G-d given ability to be successful in business. For the last twenty years or more, American businessmen have outsourced their production to foreign countries because of cheap labor. This has created a tremendous opportunity for the wide-awake person. It is possible to develop businesses and services that were left vacant.

There are many openings in the food service as in over the counter to mail order such as the diet programs that send out a month supply at a time. Manufacturing is a field that empty waiting for some smart energetic mind to fill it with productive idea. Million dollar online businesses are popping up nearly every day. Health services are a growing market.

We are not too young or old to take advantage of these wonderful opportunities. We must use our brilliant minds and take advantage of present opportunities or create new ones like other people.

Allah has blessed us and rest of humanity with the power of imagination—the ability to form a picture, story, or idea in your mind. We as human being have the value asset to think of clever and original ideas, possibilities, or solutions. This is a wonderful power. This is the same power that enabled pre-historic humans to see the movement of a rolling rock, visualize the wheel. In more modern times, we learn to fly in the same manner, by visualizing and finding the solution to make the vision a reality. Allah put everything we need in the Creation—we must go into it and bring out what we need; the same as the wood cutter or sculptor who sees an image in their mind and brings it into reality with what Allah has put in the Creation.

We developed everything in this world because Allah gave us the power of imagination and encouraged us to use it. He encourages us to find the solutions to our problems.

When it comes to business, we have the same dilemma as do the rest of the African-American community. However, we must develop business in our community as a start; we encourage the African-American community to do the same. But, we must keep in mind that it is only our start, every human being is a potential customer and the world is our marketplace.

While entering in business, we should meet all the necessary requirements that are proper and appropriate to the situation of starting and maintaining a business. Certainly, we should use caution, but, never fear. We fear only Allah. If at first, we do not succeed—— try, try again. We will not fail because Allah is with us.

We must remember that no other people in the history of mankind had to crawl up from the condition of four hundred years of slavery, brutality and cultural deprivation as did we. Judging where we came from to where we are today, we have achieved a great accomplishment. We should not be negative about our history; we should hold our heads up and march into the future in the upright position that Allah raised us.

Addressing the time and position that our community is in, knowing that through business we can finance our schools and all other community endeavors, Imam Mohammed related, "It's all about business, preaching ain't going to get it."

THIRD PRIORITY: EDUCATION

We need an Education system that is an example of academic excellence as it is shaped and formed by our Islamic perception. We must relish at the opportunity to have as independent school system that is not lacking in any area and it expresses our core philosophy (the wisdom of Imam Mohammed). This must be more than a vision; it must be as real as food on our dinner table. Every community, nation, country and serious religious organization strive to educate its own children in order maintain their way of life. Even animals teach their own; it is the responsibility of the civilized.

We cannot expect anyone else to educate our children. Allah has blessed us to come out of hundreds of years of struggle with dignity and focus on life because the Tafsir of Imam Mohammed. The future of our community awaits the actions of the present members of the community that Allah brought into existence. Although, business is our second priority, education of our children follows it because we must develop a method of funding a system as expensive as education; we thank Allah that we do not have to start from scratch.

Allah blessed Clara Muhammad with the insight and courage to start the foundation of an education system for us in the early days of the Nation of Islam. She, along with her husband, The Honorable Elijah Muhammad, established and ran the University of Islam and Muslim Girls Training. Known as the First Lady of the Nation of Islam, Sister Clara is credited with introducing her husband to the teachings of the Nation of Islam founder, W.D. Fard. In fact, it was she who guided and directed the organization during her husband's absence from 1935 to 1946. He fled death threats from rival temple leaders and was then incarcerated for sedition during World War II. She held everything together during that very crucial time.

Under her direction, The University of Islam and Muslim Girls Training schools provided education for NOI members' children. It was considered one of the nation's early versions of religious homeschooling.

Homeschooling is the education of children at home, typically by parents but sometimes by tutors. Prior to the introduction of compulsory school attendance laws, most childhood education occurred within the family or community. In fact, in early European history, it was only the wealthy who could afford to have a private tutor for their children to be taught at home. History is littered with many cultures where enlisting professional teachers or tutors were an option available only to a small elite. Sister Clara saw the significance and merit in educating our own children; therefore, she opened her home to this vital task.

Subsequently, children's attendance at the public schools was considered truancy and resulted in prosecutions and violent confrontations between Temple members and police in Detroit, Michigan and Chicago, Illinois. Courageously, she stood her ground and laid the foundation on which our education system stands today.

She passed on August 12, 1972 after a long bout with stomach cancer. When Imam Warith Deen Mohammed assumed leadership of the Nation of Islam in 1975, he renamed the University of Islam schools the Sister Clara Muhammad Schools in her honor. There are now a number of Clara Muhammad Schools across the country. Some of these schools are graduating students from high schools equipped to attend any accredited university or college in the country.

Many of them such as in Atlanta, New York, Milwaukee and several other cities serve as an example of what our school system became. The one ingredient needed for the development of a nationwide system is the proper funds. With the development of businesses in our community, we can donate the necessary funds for a uniform and quality educational system; one that would guarantee a family that moves from one part of the country, the children would continue to be received the same quality education.

FOUTH PRIORITY: GOVERNMENT

This is perhaps the easiest of all the priorities for us; we do not have to form very much. First and foremost, we thank Allah for this free and democratic society of America. The structure of America with its Constitution, Declaration of Independence, federal and state laws are very compatible with Al-Islam as it is prescribed in the Qur'an. However, there are several aspects we must establish in our community life. As we grow in our community, we will discuss and enjoin a number of them; the one the stands out most is Shuraa Baynahum (Mutual Consultation).

Allah tells us in the Qur'an about the proper conduct we should employ. He addresses different situations and what would be the best approach to respond; how we should respond to avoid great crimes; when we should defend ourselves; we should learn forgiveness and reconciliation. Most important, He encourages mutual consultation as the principle in governing our affairs. He says in Qur'an, 42:38, "Those who harken to their Lord, and establish regular prayer; who (conduct) their affairs by mutual consultation; who spend out of what We bestow upon them for substance;"

Shuraa baynahum (mutual consultation) is so important that it is placed between two of the five principles in Al-Islam; the principle of regular prayer: establishing humility as a key component; and the principle of charity; the given of one's person for a good cause such as the needy. This feature draws your attention to point that mutual consultation is the process to keep harmony and order in the society.

This process of conducting our affairs appears to be the direction Imam Mohammed was directing us to as he decentralized the Nation of Islam's organizational structure. He got us away hierarchy of rule and charismatic leaders. On some occasion, he tried to get the community to practice the concept of mutual consultation that is in the Qur'an. As time would have it, we just were not mentally or spiritually ready. However, as time will have it, times have changed.

FIFTH PRIORITY: RELIGIOUS (*MADH'HAB*)

While the other priorities are very important, it is the establishing a "school of thought" (Madh'hab) formed by the Tafsir of Imam Mohammed that will accredit or sanction our Ummah in Al-Islam. A Madh'hab addresses the time and circumstances in which a community expresses its application of the Qur'an.

At the passing of Prophet Muhammed (PBUH), the overwhelming majority of the Muslim community could not read or write. Therefore, they found themselves a community depending of the scholarship of the few. Those who could read, write or had memorized the

Qur'an and life of the Prophet were in the position to help the rest to learn. This process gave birth to the Madh'hab (plural for Madh'hab) or schools of law.

Generally, Madh'hab is a school of thought that is also termed a school of law or *fiqh* (religious jurisprudence or understanding). It is designed to protect tradition and promote understanding of Al-Islam. It is a formulation of opinions by Imams, scholars and other respected or notable persons in close association with Prophet Muhammed. The opinion usually covered interpretation of rules and laws that governed the believer's behavior. In essence, a Madh'hab is an opinion; anyone can have an opinion, but what makes it a Madh'hab is its acceptance of the people to follow it. Then, and only then, it becomes a "school."

For example, in the first 150 years of Al-Islam, there were many such "schools". In fact, several of the *Sahābah*, or contemporary "companions" of Prophet Muhammed (PBUH), are credited with founding their own. Over the years, the number of recognized Madh'hab began concentrate into areas. These Madh'hab shaped the accepted behavior and line of thinking or interpretation of the Qur'an for the majority of the Muslim population. Over time, they became fixed or standardized as rules; they became a body of law called the "Shari'ah." Each Madh'hab was a line of thinking or school of thought on the use and value of the Shari'ah. The number of "schools" varied over years as did the opinions of the founders.

Schools of law (*Madh'hab*)

Schools of law are the different Madh'hab that explains what is considered the correct application on Islamic law. As mentioned, the law is referred to as Shari'ah...in Arabic; it means "open or right way" or "path." It is found in several Ayah in the Qur'an one Ayat in particular is Al Jaathiiyah 18 "Then We put thee on the (right) Way of Religion: so follow thou that (Way). And follow not the desires of those who know not." In Al Shuuraa, it appears a number of times. Ayat 13, "He hath ordained for you that religion which He commended unto Noah." Ayat 21, "Or have they partners (of Allah) who have made lawful for them in religion that which Allah allowed not?" Of course, it is mentioned again in Ayat 38, "who (conduct) their affairs by mutual Consultation."

Most Muslims believe Shari'ah is derived from two primary sources: the Qur'an and the life example set by Prophet Muhammad. In addition, Fiqh jurisprudence is a secondary source that addresses questions that are not directly answered in the primary sources. Fiqh usually includes consensus of the religious scholars (ijmā); a deductive analogy (qiyas) from the Qur'an and life example of the Prophet. Parallel to this process, other Muslims prefer to apply reasoning ('aql). **Aql** means "intellect." This is a concept that refers to natural human knowledge as a tool of reasoning.

It is important to note, that Madh'hab do not stand alone. They can be abandoned or just not accepted by the people; thus lose its popularity. They are not to be viewed as equal or witness to the Qur'an. It is important to remember that Allah says, "He is Hafiz Qur'an," (Protector of Qur'an). Therefore, it is essential to understand that a Madh'hab neither is an opinion of the people and not a revelation from Allah nor is it protected by Him. The Qur'an stands alone, it testifies to its presence. Second only to the Qur'an is the Hadith of Prophet Muhammed (PBUH); the life of Prophet Muhammed is proof that the Qur'an can be practiced within a lifetime.

In hindsight and for the most, the intent of the Madh'hab was for the good and advancement of the religion. To that end, it is the definitive purpose of the term Madh'hab and its practical importance for the understanding of the religion that is our major concern. We are not judging them for their differences, accuracy or approval; by observing them, it may assist us to understand the need for a Madh'hab (enlighten opinion or school of thought) that defines the time in which we live as Muslims.

While there are other Madh'hab, the four that are known best by the Muslim community throughout the world are: Hanafi, Maliki, Shafi and Hanabali schools. Beginning with Imam Hanafah, this was the generation that followed the last generation of Sahaabah's (companions of the Prophet). Many of the Sahaabah's and others who knew the Prophet were very old or passed away. At the time, Imam Hanafah was a young man. He played a key role in development of the other schools.

Nu'mān ibn Thābit ibn Zuṭā ibn Marzubān, founder of the Hanafi school of Fiqh, was better known as Imam Abu Hanifah. He was born in the year 702 CE in Kufa, Iraq. He was a student of an Imam, scholar and descendent of Prophet Muhammed (PBUH) by the name of Ja'far al-Sadiq. It is reported that Muslims of Bangladesh, Pakistan, India, Afghanistan, Central Asia, Southern Russia, the Caucasus, Balkans, Turkey and parts of Iraq, all follow this Hanafi School of jurisprudence. It is also the dominant school of Muslims in the United Kingdom and Germany.

Malik ibn Anas was a student of the Imam Abu Hanifah. Imam Malik ibn Anas developed his ideas in Medina. His doctrine is in most North African and West African: Morocco, Algeria, Libya and Nigeria. Also, the Maliki Madh'hab is the official state Madh'hab of Kuwait, Bahrain and the United Arab Emirates. He was one of the teachers of Imam al-Shafi`i, the next Imam in this succession.

Muhammad ibn Idris ash-Shafi`i was a student of Malik. He taught in Iraq and then in Egypt. Muslims in Indonesia, Lower Egypt, Malaysia, Brunei, Singapore, Somalia, Kenya, Tanzania, Jordan, Lebanon, Syria, Coastal Maharashtra/Konkan and Kerala in India, Sri Lanka, Maldives, Palestine, Yemen and Kurds in the Kurdish regions follow the Shafi'i school. Al-Shafi'i placed great emphasis on the Sunnah of Muhammad, as embodied in the Hadith, as a source of the Shari'ah.

Ahmad ibn Muhammad ibn Hanbal Abu `Abd Allah al-Shaybani founded the Hanbali school, was born in Baghdad. He learned extensively from al-Shafi'i. He was an important Muslim scholar and an expert in, or student of, religious knowledge and concepts. Imam Ahmad is often referred to as the "Sheikh Ul-Islam" or the "Imam of Ahl al-Sunnah," the leading authority on the Orthodox doctrine. His school of jurisprudence is followed predominantly in the Arabian Peninsula. He personified the views of the early orthodox scholars, and in particular, the founders of the three juristic schools before him, Hanafi, Maliki and al-Shafi'i.

The followers of these four schools follow the same basic belief system but differ from one another in terms of practice and execution of rituals and in juristic interpretation of Shari'ah as conceived in Quran and Hadith. However, many Muslims consider them all equally valid.

In general, they hold that interpreting the Shari'ah to derive specific rulings (such as how to pray) is known as *Fiqh,* which literally means understanding. Additionally, they consider a Madh'hab as a particular tradition of interpreting *Fiqh.* These schools focus on specific evidence (Shafi'i and Hanbali) or general principles (Hanafi and Maliki) derived from specific evidences. The clear methodology these represent for interpreting the Shari'ah has been little change in the methodology. Change has come in the fiqh or understanding. The consensus is that the Shari'ah does not change but *fiqh* rulings change all the time.

These Madh'hab were brought into existence in the first four hundred years after the passing of Prophet Muhammed. The obvious need was for consistency and understanding of that which was bestowed on humanity by Allah through His Messenger, Prophet Muhammed.

It has been nearly a thousand years since the work of these great Imams. That great enlighten knowledge brought to the world is adrift like a ship without a rudder in the ocean of time. The world has awakened and responded to that great knowledge, but the bearers of the wisdom have fallen asleep in the token of time.

Europeans have come out of the dark ages and industrialized the earth. China has become a giant in the economy of the world. India and Japan have level the field of technology. The world is not just spinning around on its axis, it is moving forward on the back of progress.

The most important phenomenon of all the events is the fact that the African-American people are a new people or social group that did not exist a thousand years ago. There are over seventeen million of us; that is about that same number of Jewish people throughout the world. We don't think or act as Jews, Arabs or Caucasians. We are a new people in a world that is changing very fast.

As fast as people come into Al-Islam, the confusion of old ways and new ideas clash on the battle fields of reality leaving a trail of blood to the doorsteps of the future.

As it was in the beginning, so shall it be in the end. The need for understanding has come again to humanity. The source of this understanding is coming through a virgin community that is not known to the world-a community of knowledge and wisdom of the scripture—a community that has not been visited by a prophet.

The world will witness a virgin birth; Allah, in the Tafsir of Imam Mohammed, has created a new Madh'hab—a particular tradition or methodology of interpreting *Fiqh in America out of the African-American community*. He has prepared Imam Mohammed to understand Qur'an, Bible and life example of Prophet Muhammed (PBUH), and how to apply that understanding in today's world. With this knowledge, Imam Mohammed has given birth to the community that will light up the world of understanding with the Tafsir of Imam Mohammed.

As it were the responsibility of the scholars of past to develop Madh'hab, it is our duty to establish this all important fifth priority in our community structure of Al-Islam. We must gather and categorize the Tafsir of Imam Mohammed into a Madh'hab as a school of thought. It will be our vision of reality through his Madh'hab that will be able to use as a guide.

We must form committees of Imams, scholars, instructors, families, friends and all the learned men and women who lived their daily lives committed to the Tafsir of Imam Mohammed to develop the insight that he had on any given subject, and develop them into a school of thought—a Madh'hab.

Additionally, it is absolutely necessary that the Imams, who were in association with Imam Mohammed, wrote and delivered lectures, khubars and talks with Imam Mohammed's language began to organize and publish their lectures in the form of books for the world.

As an Imam of Imam Mohammed, your lectures constitute the characteristic and profound effect and influence of Imam Mohammed's language. While your lectures are not more important than the language and each Imam had his own personality, it is your valued uniqueness in your lectures that makes the language what it is.

These books would not be so important for our community, but they are essential for "Dawah" (spreading the word to others). What maybe redundant to our community is fresh and new knowledge for the world. We cannot leave this for anyone else to do. After the fact and the dust have cleared, many will try to take credit and canonize Imam Mohammed's work. We cannot leave this for the institutions, scholars (Muslim or non-Muslim), or anyone else outside of our community—those people who were respectful supporters and admirers, but were not overtly devoted to the daily activities of the community and Imam Mohammed's insight. We certainly cannot leave it in the hands of those who opposed Imam Mohammed and his views.

Without question or hesitation, we must produce thousands of books—Imams and those who believe as we believe. This job must be done by us—those who lived his views daily. It must be done with our hands, from our mind and founded on our experience. Allah did not bring us into existence to stand on the sideline and watch humanity parade by into the horizon of progress. These publications along with the establishment of Imam Mohammed's Madh'hab are our responsibility ordained on us by Allah.

When Imam Mohammed was asked about his position on the idea of new Madh'hab in America by Dr. Lawrence Mamlya in an interview, he replied, "I'm more strongly holding to that belief now than I was several years ago when I first mentioned it." He continued to express the need as he said, "We are in a very new human society. We need to study the old Madh'hab in lieu of all the changes in the world." As he continued his line of reasoning, he was very definite about the transformation of the African under the condition of slavery in America into a new people as he said, "G-d has created us again. He restored the human life and put it into this human vessel again." As he concluded, he emphasized, "We are a new people; we did not exist before; why should the Islamic world be deprived of Islam being expressed through a new and innocent vessel."

Spirit of Bilal

CHAPTER 19

ACCEPTING THE MISSION

Allah has blessed our community with a special knowledge that establishes us in a defining moment in history—the moment when the old world ends and the new world begins. This historical moment will identify us as a community of light (knowledge for the world), and the first generation born to establish the new world created on the spirit of human excellence; the same spirit that was promised in scripture and exemplified in the original community established by Prophet Muhammed 1,400 years ago.

To understand this concept, it is necessary to know that the word "world" in scripture is addressing the attitude and mental disposition of those who control source and quality knowledge to create a body of "information" in the secular world. In return, that "information" will produce the behavior in people because it is designed to shape their minds.

"Information" is a "concept word" that is packed with power. Its practical meaning begins with its parts; the "in" stands for enter; the "form" represents shaping, determining or influence; the suffix "tion" is the act of doing something. Simply, information means the knowledge or data that enters a situation shapes the outcome. In sociological and psychological terms, it means, "The Knowledge which enters the mind shapes the disposition of the mind; thus, causing the behavior of the individual or population that receive it to be defined by it." This is the same idea that Imam Mohammed expressed when he said, "Words make people."

Therefore, understanding the concept that "words make people," it is easier to comprehend the idea when scripture is addressing the concept of world (good or bad), it is defining the disposition of the people and the knowledge that shaped their behavior. In other words, it is identifying the secular world, its formation and behavior.

The present world we live is old secular world. According to scripture, it is the world that was established with the corrupted knowledge from Shaitan (The Devil or Satan) that influenced it. Satan's knowledge is a corruption of Allah's Truth and a false light that is designed to shape and mislead human behavior to be adverse to the plan of Allah. As a result of the devil meddling and interfering with humanity's society—the secular world, Allah established the correct knowledge (light) in a new community that He raised to illuminate the secular world with His knowledge (embodied in the insights of Imam Mohammed) to expose Satan's false knowledge; thus ushering out the old world (way of thinking) and bringing in the new.

The knowledge that Allah established in the new community is not a new knowledge. It is the same that the prophets received thousands of years ago. What made it seem different is time and the growth of the intellect in the masses of the people. Humanity has grown in its understanding of our physical, sociological and psychological environment.

Over thousands of years, the human family has developed many words and languages such as Arabic, Spanish, English, mathematics and many others to include computer-generated idiom and lingo; these languages and words assist us in studying and expressing what we find in our environment. Also, they make it possible for humanity to understand the concepts that were revealed in scripture.

Now that humanity has grown, Allah just inspires one of us as "His Witness" to sincerely study and trust that Allah will guide him. That one, after grasping the concepts that reveal the plan of Allah, will inspire the rest; thus forming a community with that understanding and inspiration. In return, the community will bring that understanding to light and inspire the world.

The core of the new secular world will be based on striving for human excellence. As it advances scientifically and materially, it will have human salvation as its interest in common; human excellence will become the goal, and Moral Courage as the key to achieve the goal.

As the community of light for the world, we must be very careful that we do not make same mistake as did those other communities of light.

The secular world was not created to be bad or evil; it was directed off the course that Allah put it on. Out of his mercy, Allah has raised communities of light as a warning with the duty to bring the knowledge to the secular world to guide it back to the straightway. But, the philosophies and life styles of the secular world should not be adapted by the community.

The community is instructed by Allah that they should only follow His direct knowledge and not mix it with the knowledge of the world. Unfortunately, this is a task that the communities before us failed to keep.

We, the community born out of the African-American experience, stand at the same threshold as did those religious communities of the past. As a reminder to us and a lesson from which we can learn, they chose a course that proved to be a breakdown between them and the message they received from Allah. As a result of this blunder, they are divided and confused. Subsequently, the world has distorted the religious guidance...it is in spiritual darkness and befuddlement. The evidence of their mistake is locked in history. The parade of this huge error began with the Israelites.

THE LACK OF FAITH: Long before the Israelites were known as the Jewish community, they followed the word of The Lord (Al-Rabb) as it was reflected to them by Prophets. Al-Rabb (The Lord) was one of the earliest known attributes of Allah used by religious communities. The prophets were not leaders in the secular world's concept. They were reflections of The Lord's Word to those who would believe. Therefore, this suggests that the community was actually followers of the Creator's Word, and not the individual prophet in terms of his personal opinion or concepts.

The Biblical historians give the Israelites the distinction as being the first in the succession of those communities that received the Word. Yet, with divine direction as

235

their guide, the Israelites felt that this was not enough for them to accept their status in the world. They wanted to take on some of the characteristics of the secular world...they wanted a king to rule over them as other nations. Their story is revealed in the Qur'an in Suurah Al Baqarah, Ayat 246-247. It is also in the Holy Bible in 1 Samuel 8: 5-20.

The Qur'an, in Al Baqarah in Ayah 246, states. "Hast thou not Turned thy vision to the Chiefs of the Children of Israel after (the time of) Moses? They said to a prophet (That was) among them: "Appoint for us a king that we may fight in the cause of Allah."

This discourse continued in Ayah 247, "Their Prophet said to them: "(Allah) hath appointed Talut as king over you." Clearly, Allah gave the desire; however, they still were not satisfied with Allah's direction. The Ayah states, "They said: "How can he exercise authority over us when we are better fitted than he to exercise authority, and he is not even gifted, with wealth in abundance?" It seems that Allah's choice just was not good enough for them.

While the Qur'an is straight forward by showing that it was the people who requested a secular world structure that began their downfall. There is also a description of the situation that is in the Bible in *1 SAMUEL 8: 5-20.*

The discussion and request was very similar to the one in the Qur'an. However, there were condemning words as Allah spoke to them in these words, "And the LORD said unto Samuel: 'Hearken unto the voice of the people in all that they say unto thee; for they have not rejected thee, but they have rejected me, that I should not be reign over them." This is perhaps the most damaging and condemning statement that defines their sin for taking their position. This points out that the Israelites turned away from Allah as characterized by their foolish request. In essence, the act of wanting leadership other than Allah is rejecting Allah; the head of a community of light must be the Word of Allah...not an individual or group. In return for this action of the Israelites, Allah no longer guided them.

From that point, as you trace the history of the Israelites, starting with Talut (Saul) their history was littered with a succession of kings was accompanied with corruption and a breakdown in the social fabric of their society. They waged war against each other. Death and destruction was their companion. Furthermore, as a consequence of their actions, their people were eventually dominated by another nation. By inviting the traditions of the structure of secular society into the way of life, they gain the world (Its Ways) and lost the soul (the life that Allah gave them).

They had gotten so far off the path that by the time of the Prophet Jesus (Isa), they could not be considered the children of Allah's Word even though they were seeds of Abraham. The account of this fact is in the Bible in St. John 8: verses 37-44.

Prophet Jesus began by saying, "I know that ye are Abraham's seed; but ye seek to kill me, because my word hath no place in you."He continued in verse 39, "If ye were Abraham's children, ye would do the works of Abraham." There is a strong distinction as the difference between the meaning of seed and children...they are not the same. As the Prophet argued with them, he brought it to a peak in verse 44 as he stated, "Ye are of your father the devil, and lusts of your father ye will do. He was a murderer from the beginning, and abode not in the truth, because there is no truth in him. When he speakeeth a lie, he speakeeth of his own: for he is a liar, and the father of it."

In that defining moment of their history, their community changed from honorable status to the lowest possible position in history...they had transformed into materialist. They did not evolve spiritually; they were locked in the concept that heaven and hell was only in the present material world. Although Jesus used the term devil; they had neither a real idea of the concept nor a belief in life after the physical death. They changed from a community of light directed by the spirit and malformed into a community of darkness craving for material wealth. They began to operate on "distorted truth" (darkness) to gain control of the material world until the Day of Judgment (the resurrection of the Truth / Light). Even today, in the eyes of the world, Israel is considered a police state; not an example of truth or religious guidance. Most important, it is the consequent of their choice that began when they requested a king in place of Allah's reign.

THE HIJACK: The community of light following the Israelites was the one that Isa (Jesus of Nazareth) raised with Allah's permission; it did not do much better. Unlike the Israelites, their undoing was not because they had a lack of faith in divine guidance; it was due to two elements that weaken the foundation established by Jesus. The foundation that Jesus laid was the concept of "faith" and "love." This can be found in the Bible in Mathew 4:5 as he said, "It is written, Man shall not live by bread alone, but by every word that proceedeth out of the mouth of GOD." This was pointed out again in *2 Corinthians 3:6*, "... not of the letter, but of the spirit: for the letter killeth, but the spirit giveth life." His focus was on their spiritual development. In essence, he taught that the word of Allah would be the leadership of the community. By the time he returned to Allah, he had instructed his community of light that he was in them, and they in him, and they all were one with the Creator; he did not name any individuals the successor to lead his community. He left the community with a great sense of empowerment which is reflected in the Bible in St. John 14:17 as he said, "Even the Spirit of Truth; whom the world cannot receive, because it seeth him not, neither knoweth him: but ye know him; for he dwelleth with you, and shall be in you." He continued this powerful point in verse 20 as he said, "At that day ye shall know that I am in my Father, and ye are in me, and I in you." It is clear that Allah's word is in the person as their guide; the community was left on the right path.

Like the Israelites, this new community was formed with the word of Allah. However, unlike them, Jesus' community wasn't seeking to be like the secular world. In fact, they like Jesus were in the world but not of the world. They did not want to be like the secular world; it was not side-tracked as much as the movement was taken over. This take-over came by way of weak elements that assumed leadership for the community, namely, Peter and Paul.

Peter and Paul were two personalities in Biblical history that shaped the modern day Christianity. Ironically, they were the weakest of the community. In fact, Jesus said that Peter was of little faith, yet the church would be built on him.

Paul's original name was Saul. He wasn't supporter of Jesus...he persecuted Jesus' followers. After Jesus passed, they were predominant figures in the movement. It was he and Peter who named the community "Christians." According the Bible Acts 11: 26, discussing Paul, it said, "And when he had found him, he brought him unto An'tioch. And it came to pass, that a whole year they assembled themselves with the church, and taught much people. And the disciples were called Christians first in Antioch." This was after Jesus had passed, and only the beginning of their historic influence on the community Jesus left behind.

From this point, they began to build Christianity; A Christianity that altered the original ideas Jesus had established; the philosophy allowed the secular world to take complete control of the religious message. It was through this door that Pagan worship, German and Greek philosophies and superstitions entered the Christian foundation. While discussing the effect of some of these concepts such as Gnostics, Marcionite position, author Ninian Smart, in his book "The Religious Experience of Mankind, said, "By destroying this monotheistic basis of the Christian faith such doctrines allowed entry to all kinds of extraneous mythological ideas." Concepts such as Christmas, Easter and the worship of "Saints," are just a few false ideas that are associated with Jesus and his original teachings. The belief in One G-d (monotheism) as taught by Jesus was distorted to the point of Shirk (Associating Partners with Allah). The gate of corruption was opened by Paul and Peter.

Paul's, who called himself the "Apostle to the Gentiles", influence on Christian thinking arguably, has been more significant than any other New Testament author. According to the Acts of the Apostles, his conversion (or metanoia) took place on the road to Damascus, where he experienced a vision of the resurrected Jesus after which he was temporarily blinded. Unlike Jesus' apostles in Jerusalem, Paul had not known Jesus in person. Paul asserted that he received the Gospel not from man, but by the revelation of Jesus Christ, Paul claimed almost total independence from the "mother church" in Jerusalem. Christianity is commonly said to owe as much to Paul as to Jesus.

Thirteen epistles in the New Testament of the Bible are traditionally attributed to Paul, of whom seven are considered absolutely genuine, three are decidedly not from Paul, and the other three are in dispute, according to most religious scholars. They also concluded that Paul apparently dictated all his epistles through a secretary (or amanuensis). These epistles were circulated within the Christian community, where they were read aloud in church along with other works. Paul's epistles were accepted early as scripture and later established as Canon of Scripture (an authentic list of books accepted as Holy Scripture). Canon is synonymous to Law.

Paul declared that faith in Christ made the Torah unnecessary for salvation, exalted the Christian church as the body of Christ, and depicted the world outside the Church as under judgment. Augustine's foundational work on the gospel as a gift (grace), on morality as life in the Spirit, on predestination, and on original sin all derives from Paul, especially Romans. Martin Luther expressed Paul's doctrine of faith most strongly as justification by faith alone. John Calvin developed Augustine's predestination into double predestination. Karl Barth's commentary on the Letter to the Romans had a political as well as theological impact. In the East, church fathers reduced the element of election in Romans 9 to divine fore knowledge, as have the

Western humanists. These scholars are expressing the fact that the modern concepts in Christianity are due to Paul.

Peter, on the other hand, dissimilar from Paul, had more of a structural influence on the shaping of Christianity, especially as it relates to its hierarchy. Primacy of Simon Peter is a reference given to Peter. Primacy is the dominance or predominance established under Peter. A number of Christian denominations and scholars hold that Simon Peter was the most prominent of the apostles, favored by Jesus of Nazareth with the first place of honor and authority. This doctrine is known as the Primacy of Simon Peter or the Petrine Primacy (from the Latin Petrus = Peter). A number of traditions, most notably Roman Catholic but others as well, hold that Simon Peter, also known as Saint Peter or Cephas, was the first Bishop of Antioch, the first Bishop of Rome, and was a martyr during the persecution of the emperor Nero. The early Christian church at that time, however, did not have the same precisely delineated functions for bishops or other official roles that one can find today. Nevertheless, it is obvious that this was the beginning of the "Hierarchy" in that religious community; a pecking order.

This Primacy of Peter is closely related to, and indeed essential to, the Papal Primacy, that is, the idea that the papacy, by divine institution, enjoys delegated authority from Jesus over the entire Church. However, this doctrine of the Roman Catholic Church makes a distinction between the personal prestige of Peter and the supremacy of the office of pope which Catholics believe Jesus instituted in the person of Peter. Other denominations hold that the primacy of Peter was only relevant during the lifetime of Peter. There are various views on the nature of the primacy and how it was exercised.

The reasons for the nature of the primacy are complex, hinging upon matters of doctrine, history, and politics. The debate is often reduced to a discussion of the meaning and translation of verse 18 of chapter 16 of the Gospel of Matthew, the "on this rock" passage. That passage is: "And I say also unto thee, that thou art Peter, and upon this rock I will build my church; and the gates of hell shall not prevail against it." (King James Version)

In the language that Jesus spoke, the same word, "כֵּיפָא" (cepha), was used for both Peter's name and for the rock on which Jesus said he would build his church. Protestant view on the Matthew verse agrees with the

Roman Catholic view about primacy stem from doctrinal sources as those over the identification of Simon Peter with the Pope.

It is very important for us to be grateful to Allah for Imam Mohammed. With his Tafsir, we can look into history and see the mistakes of those that came before us. It is clear that they misunderstood that verse. Especially when you consider the few verses that came before and after it.

According to King James Version, Jesus was talking with the disciples about who people were saying he was. Then in verse 15, Jesus asks them, "But who say ye that I am?" The following verse 16 states, "And Simon Peter answered and said, Thou art the Christ, the Son of the living God." In 17, Jesus replied, "And Jesus answered and said unto him, Blessed art thou, Simon Barjona: for flesh and blood hath not revealed it unto thee, but my Father which in heaven." The next verse 18 is the one in question, "And I say also unto thee, That thou art Peter, and upon this rock I will build my church; and the gates of hell shall not prevail against it."

What is obvious in today's light, Jesus was not talking about "flesh and blood" it was "Faith." Once you substitute Faith for Peter, its common sense that his community was to be established on faith in the Creator and not just the letter of the law. Jesus in the next few verses opened the eyes of the disciples to this important point.

He charged them not to tell anyone who he was. According to verse 21, He began to demonstrate things to them; it reads, "From that time forth began Jesus to shew unto his disciples, how that he must go unto Jerusalem, and suffer many things of the elders and chief priests and scribes and be killed, and be raised again the third day." In the very next verse 22, it says, "Then Peter took him, and began to rebuke him, saying, Be it far from thee, Lord: this shall not be unto thee." Here, Peter is actually reprimanding Jesus. Verse 23, should have opened their eyes as it says, "But he turned, and said unto Peter, Get thee behind me, Satan: thou art an offence unto me: for thou savoures not the things that be of God, but those that be of men." Jesus referred to Peter as Satan...not only is this a condemnation on Peter's character, it shows that Satan will be in the high places in religion.

These verses show the extreme nature of the human being. On one hand, with faith, the future of the human family can be established on him. While, on the other hand, he can be humanity's worst enemy because of the lack of faith. Nevertheless, as the story goes, it was

Peter who took this opportunity to build his concept and structure of what he thought the religious community should be.

The reason why the Roman Church had been accorded an incontestable precedence over all other apostolic churches was that its Petrine and Pauline 'apostolicity' was in fact added to the city's position as the capital city, and only the conjunction of both of these elements gave the Bishop of Rome the right to occupy the place of a primate in the Christian world with the consensus of all the churches.

Peter's efforts, in conjunction with Paul's, seized and commanded the religious community that Jesus began; they hijacked the community with their messages and organizations that corrupted the original concept. The community became filled with pagan ideology; even more damaging it allowed the secular structure of hierarchy to become the framework of the church. From the Pope and his priests to the small storefront churches with their preachers and their deacon boards, this hierarchy structure rules the religious massages and separate them from Allah as intercessors. Furthermore, it is this community some whom are poor that financially support this arrangement; and it is the one at the top of the structure getting the bulk of the money for their private use. This process has gotten the religious community so far off course that it can't possibly put humanity on the right path.

The lesson to be learned from this hijacking of the religious community is vigilance. We must be very watchful of those individuals or groups, inside and outside of our community, which lay in wait for the opportunity to takeover and become the leaders of our community, or divide it into segments. The story of Solomon depicts an example of a true believer as appose to one who is willing to sacrifice the life of the community.

The scripture speaks of two women claiming to be the baby's mother. In his wisdom, Solomon ordered to cut the baby into two parts, given each women a part. One woman agreed to the order; while the other women said "NO" give the whole living baby to the other women. At that moment Solomon knew that the real mother would rather give her baby away before she would see it die. We will be confronted with people of that selfish mentality who want to divide the community just to serve their ego to be a leader.

Other than Prophet Muhammed, we must realize that we have had the greatest religious teacher in history in the person of Imam Mohammed. We have been spiritually fed and we are full. No one else can take us further; it is we who must take the world further. We were students of Imam Mohammed; now we are students of the Qur'an and teachers of the world. However, history still has a lesson for us.

MISINTERPRETATION: Prophet Muhammed had established a new community as a result of following the word of Allah revealed to him in the Holy Qur'an. This new community engulfed the entire peninsula of Arabia. It had been tried and tested with war, patience and obedience. It had one more hurdle to cross. It was on Mount Arafat in his last Sermon that Prophet Muhammed addressed this issue.

He addressed several critical concerns, each very vital. He said, "Beware of Satan, for the safety of your religion. He has lost all hope that he will ever be able to lead you astray in big things, so beware of following him in small things." This concern is liken to the fish bone...it is always the small one that gets stuck in your throat because you don't see it. Satan is trying to lead man...he is focused on the small matters to lead the community astray. He is trying to prove to Allah that man is not worthy of Allah's attention, and that he is better to lead.

The Prophet was making the community aware and guard against the small issues because they may matter most. Satan is associated with leadership. The word is not a trick, guide or influence...it is lead.

Imam Mohammed mentioned that Satan wants to rule and be over man. This is the main reason no one in their right mind wants to be the leader over Allah's community. Satan wants to dominate; this is a clear and very important point.

Another vital point Prophet Muhammed (PBUH) made on that day was when he stated, "O People, NO PROPHET OR APOSTLE WILL COME AFTER ME AND NO NEW FAITH WILL BE BORN. Reason well, therefore, O People, and understand words which I convey to you. I leave behind me two things; the Qur'an and my life example the Sunnah and if you follow these you will never go astray." This powerful declaration confirms two most important objectives.

First, it establishes complete Autonomy; unconditional freeing of the individual to respond to his Lord without an intercessor. It puts everyone on the same page...no big 'I's' and little 'you's.' Everyone has the same information. No individual needs to wait or look for someone else to lead or instruct them. Everyone is able and entitled to follow the word of Allah on their own!

Second, by understanding the first objective, your salvation is guaranteed! In conclusion, the individual as well as community should be guided by the word of Allah. The word must be applied in the daily lives of the believers.

This was the directions the Prophet left his Ummah (community). However, as soon as he passed, the Muslim community took a different position. Consciously or unconsciously, they felt that this was not enough. They fell into the same mistake as the Israelites did a few thousand years earlier. They wanted flesh and blood to lead them...the Qur'an was not sufficient; they fell back onto secular world thinking.

In the secular world, a hierarchy structure is necessary...they have leaders, presidents, kings, queens, shahs, amirs to assist them in organizing and controlling people. Whereas, in Allah's community, there is complete freedom. Freedom of choice is a necessity. It is a natural behavior created in the human being by Allah. And all structures should follow this natural order. Hierarchies have tendency to obstruct this order. The religious community must follow Allah directly. There are no intercessors between him and his community or the individuals in the community. Therefore, there are no such concepts of a hierarchy in the religious community established by Allah through his Prophets; there is the word of Allah and each individual must follow it according to their own understanding!

Everyone should follow Allah's word exclusively. However, immediately after the passing of Prophet Muhammed (PBUH), the Muslim community decided to establish a leader. The community began to argue and divide. They separated in groups and over time into sects. They developed a Shari'ah (Law) and Fiqh, and as history indicates, they called the leader a Caliphate or Khilaafa.

The caliphate (from the Arabic خلافة or khilāfa) represented the political leadership of the Muslim Ummah in classical and medieval Islamic history and juristic theory. The head of state's position (caliph) is based on the notion of a successor to Prophet Muhammed's authority. This was their misinterpretation. It was not one given to them by the Prophet.

One of their opinions was derived from Ayyat 55 in Suurah Al Nur. It says, "Allah has promised, to those among you who believe and work righteous deeds, that He will, of a surety, grant them in the land, inheritance (Of power), As He granted it to those before them; that

He will establish in authority their religion-the one which He has chosen for them; and that He will change (their state), after the fear in which they (lived). To one of security and peace: They will worship Me (alone) and not associate aught with Me.' If they do reject Faith after this, they are rebellious and wicked." It is important to note that the words (of power), (their state) and (alone) are not in the Arabic of the Qur'an. The Abdullah Yusuf Ali version uses these words to have you understand what he thinks this Ayyat meant.

Certainly, we have the advantage of hindsight and the Tafsir of Imam Warith Deen Mohammed, but, it is clear that it is the religion that will gain respect in the society. Allah will make religious community reputable and well known as he established earlier communities such as The Israelites.

There were different opinions as to who that leader would be. In fact, the divisions in the community became more obvious and combated. When Bilal Ibn Rabba was asked to lead, he refused the offer. Keep in mind, in addition to being the one who called the Adhan (call Muslims to prayer); he was considered one of the most sincere followers of Prophet Muhammed. After he refused leadership, they continued their search.

As the community divided into groups, over time, their attitude varied along with the formation of the groups. For example, Sunni dictates that the caliph should be selected by Shura, elected by Muslims or their representatives. Whereas, the followers of Shia believe the caliph was an Imam descended in a line from the Ahl al-Bayt. The internal dispute over who was to succeed Ja'far as Imam led to schism within Shi'a Islam. This is a few of the many differences compared to the number of sects and schools of thought that surfaced after the passing of the Prophet.

From the time of Muhammad (PBUH) passed until 1924, there were the Sunni, Shi'ah, Hanafi, Maliki, Sufi, Khawaarij, Salafi, Ahmadiyya and many others groups and sects claiming their legitimacy as either the only successor to the Prophet or true inheritors of the faith. The caliphate was the only form of governance that had full approval of that time. The caliph, or head of state, was often known as Amir al-Mu'minin (أم ير ال مؤم ذ ين) "Commander of the Believers", Imam al-Ummah, Imam al-Mu'minīn (ال مؤم ذ ين إمام), or more colloquially, leader of all the Muslims. At times there may have been rival claimant caliphs in different parts of the Islamic world, and divisions between the Shi'a and Sunni parts.

Sunni Muslims consider Abu-Bakr to be the first legitimate Caliph, while Shi'a considered Ali to have been the first truly legitimate Caliph who eventually sanctioned Abu-Bakr. This was a sign of the following tragedies.

Abu Bakr, the first successor of the Prophet (PBUH), nominated Umar as his successor on his deathbed, and there was consensus in the Muslim community to his choice. Umar Ibn Khattab, the second caliph was killed by a slave. His successor, Uthman Ibn Affan, was killed by members of a apposing group. Ali then took control; he had two major rebellions and was assassinated after a tumultuous rule of only five years. This period is known as the Fitna, and the community could not mend their philosophical difference; they remain fragmented.

As it relates to that time of turmoil and mayhem, during one of his lectures, Imam Warith Deen Mohammed pointed out that he believed that all this killing and confusion was an indication that the Muslim community should not have a Khalifa as a leader or establish a leadership role of Khalifas. He discussed this in a lecture saying, "Now I'm going to say something that I haven't said before but that I wanted to say a million times. There is a sign in the short life of the khalifas. I think only one of them had what you might call a normal, long life. There is a sign there for us. And we would be fools not to take it as a sign. After the passing of the Prophet, khalifas, rulers, were betrayed, assassinated, one behind the other. Their lives were not long with the people, except for one, and really his wasn't too long. That is a sign." In conjunction with that opinion, this was compounded a divisive mentality. Muslim began to separate themselves by placing other words in front of the word Muslim; this labeling practice carried with it the philosophy "I am right and better than you." Sunni, Shi'ah, Hanafi, Maliki, Sufi, Khawaarij, Salafi, Ahmadiyya and many others terms were used to proceed the word Muslim, creating different sects, each identifying that it was the correct way, and the others were wrong. Each knew that Allah and His messengers call them "Muslim" with no prefix or suffix; there is no label that could improve upon Allah's word, "Muslim." In Surah 30 Ayat 32, Allah says, "Those who split up their Religion, and become Sects—each party rejoicing in that which is with itself!" This is followed in Surah 42:13 where Allah commanded the Believers not to divide; It says, "the same religion has He established for you as that which He enjoined on Noah—That which We have sent by inspiration to thee—And that which We enjoined on Abraham, Moses, and Jesus: Namely, that ye should remain steadfast in Religion, and make No divisions therein:..." In the next Ayah, the Qur'an continued, "And they became divided only after knowledge reached them—through selfish envy as between themselves." These Ayat are inclusive of all religion that received revelations from Allah.

Every label was divisive in its nature or innovation. They invented labels from terms of their own concoction that they used out of context; they were not labels revealed by Allah or promoted by any of His Messengers to cause division in the community. Even today Muslims who are descendents of that era and methodology are still fighting and killing each other because of these labels with their inbred philosophies of division; there is still Fitna (turmoil and trouble) between these communities. Had they just used "Muslim" as did Allah and His Messengers they may not have a world filled with brother against brother. We must accept Allah's guidance in the Qur'an and the life example of Prophet Muhammed that we are known as "Muslim;" anything else is an innovation.

Also, as students of history, we should recognize that in three different situations of the religious communities (Israelites, Christians and Muslims) altered or were distracted from the original purpose. The first community demonstrated a lack of faith in the case of the Israelites. This was followed by the philosophical hijacking of Jesus' community known today as Christians. As the final straw, the total lack of understanding due to misinterpretations shown by the Muslim community as they took the different position on leadership and successor to Prophet Muhammed (PBUH). Each community went from one guided by Allah to one led by men.

Although Allah established them as a community separate from worldly influences, each of them changed their makeup to that of the secular world. Allah raised them to be balanced and an example to the rest of mankind (the secular world). But, they became an integrated or functioning part of the secular world. And in each case, they failed the final test...what to do after the prophet passed.

This is perhaps the most important illustration in history that we must consider as to our situation. We find ourselves in the same dilemma that the Israelites, Jesus's community and Muslims faced; they made a huge mistake because their prophet was aging or returned to Allah. Some of us, after the passing of Imam Mohammed, want someone to lead us; while others of us believe that Allah is enough.

Some of us indicate that all creatures lead themselves as we point to the animal kingdom as an example that has one out front leading the rest. This occurs in a pack or group such as the case of flock of birds flying south, a pack of wolves hunting for food or a herd of antelopes migrating thousands of miles across the dry plains into an area where there is water.

Still others point to the fact that organizations, associations and nations have leaders. It is easily conceivable that Allah permits the animal kingdom and the secular world to have this kind of leadership.

This is the foundation of the argument made by the Israelites. They wanted that type of leadership for their community. Theirs was an obvious wrong; we can't follow in the footsteps of those who do wrong.

It is also just as conceivable that in the case of the religious community, Allah commands us to follow His word, and not each other. This process will protect us from the tragedy that beset a herd of wild animals that when its leader goes over a cliff and falls into the canyon the herd will blindly plunge to their death after him. Or, in the case of a zealous secular leader that leads his country into a mindless war killing thousands of innocent people as in the case Adolf Hitler. This is not isolated to governments as we refer to religious leaders killing thousands of people as in the murder suicide committed by Jim Jones. History is also laced with these tragic outcomes. They serve as an excellent example of what not to do. Allah's word is our refuge; we must trust it.

We must be mindful of the fact that each human being is autonomous: a self-governed individual. "Each tub must set on its own bottom" is the concept that instructs the only way that each of us can be independently responsible for our behavior.

This is more emphatic in a religious community because we must also correct each other or as the Qur'an puts it, "call our brother back from his wrong." We have the responsibility to self-correct and help others. This is only when individuals have the power to follow Allah's word to the best of his or her ability. This is a distinguishing factor between animals and the human being.

Spirit of Bilal

CHAPTER 20

ORGANIZING LIFE

Although, we are the example, there are certain aspects about the society that will assist our community design; however, we cannot be a carbon copy of the society and its habits. Having complete knowledge of the errors of the religious communities that came before us, we must proceed with a measure of prudence. For instance, the society in many cases is very organized and efficient. This increases their productivity. They have economical, political, educational and other social groups that are formed into associations, organizations and corporations. These structures are task oriented; therefore, these small but effective units make the greater body operate efficiently.

Imam Mohammed said, "We need organization as much as we need religion." He also made an emphatic point that we had to respect our autonomy—each center and Masajid must be self-governed. He defined this concept in these words, "You have to continue to be responsible for the administration for your own Centers or Mosque or businesses or whatever you have." This was an element in the decentralization process he desired for our community. He had seriously devoted himself and persevered to completely ending central or national control of an individual or group over the community.

Autonomy will protect our community from small minded, self-centered, power seeking individuals who want to control the community with their selfish objectives. They do not realize that each Masajid, center and individual has been freed by Imam Mohammed to follow Allah and the life example of Prophet Muhammed on their own.

With these thoughts as our back-drop, how do we maintain our autonomy and achieve organization? The answer to this question lies in our understanding of organization and its purpose.

There is a tremendous need for organizations as internal functions within the community. A community functions best when it has smaller organizations headed up by like-minded people to complete a specific task that they formed to achieve.

In simple terms, an organization is the bringing parts together into an orderly form. Technically, organization is a term that references an administrative function. It is the structure within associations, businesses, corporations or any group that assist the orderly function for their administrative, managerial, directorial, executive, governmental and decision-making procedures; it assists the task oriented operation. In fact, in terms of performance, its name and function originates from a task driven apparatus—the organ. It is the same organ that is found in the human body and other living creatures.

In biology, it is a group of tissues that perform a specific function or group of functions. Usually there is a main tissue and sporadic (irregular or infrequent) tissues. The main tissue is the one that is unique for the specific organ. For example, main tissue in the heart is the myocardium, while sporadic are the nerves, blood, connective etc. A grouping of tissues into a distinct structure, as a heart or kidney, in humans and other animals performs a specialized task. Each organ has a different function. The heart's primary task is to pump blood; whereas, the kidney has a different function.

Our community is a body with the word of Allah as it head, Qur'an as its guide, life of Prophet Muhammed as its example and the Tafsir of Imam Mohammed as its light of understanding. For clearness, picture our Ummah in the form of a human body. The body consists of all those who believe and live the Tafsir of Imam Mohammed; that is the unique quality of the Ummah. The head is the word of Allah (the Qur'an) and Life example of Prophet Muhammed (PBUH); that is what makes us part of the worldwide Muslim Ummah. Let us compare our Ummah to the human body.

The human body has appendages such as the legs, arms and other valuable parts; as valuable as they are to the balance and quality of life, if the body loss one of any of them, the body is still alive. For example, to lose a leg, arm or any appendage is a troubled experience. However, the body, in most cases, is still alive; it can live without most appendages. On the other hand, the loss of or even damage to an organ such as the heart, lung, kidney or liver would not only affect the quality of life, it can mean death in most cases; we cannot live without organs. We must replace them or depart this life. The organs are so important to life that the word organism means life or something that is or was alive.

Getting back to Imam Mohammed's words, "We need organization as much as we need religion," it becomes obvious that our survival as an Ummah depends on how well we develop organizations within our Ummah.

We do not need someone or a group as the leader, head or spokesperson of our Ummah because the word of Allah (Qur'an) is the head; to help us to understand this point, Allah gave us the life of Prophet Muhammed (PBUH). We cannot change or improve on Allah's word.

This is point that Allah made to the Israelites; unfortunately for them, they did not understand. This answers the other point that Imam Mohammed made about autonomy as he said, "G-d wants each of us to have as much respect for our own intelligence to be responsible for our own behavior." Therefore, we do not need someone over us telling what they think regarding our behavior; especially, since we all have the same information from Allah, Prophet Muhammad (PBUH) and Imam Mohammed, give or take a word or two.

Unlike the time of the Prophet when he and the Sahaabah's had to memorize the Qur'an to teach it to others, we do not have to employ that process as the prime source of spreading the words of the Qur'an. Because of technology and education, humanity has gone through the adolescent growth period in human society. In an educated society, most people can read and write; they also have access to technology that enables them to educate themselves in a matter of minutes, days or months in language and battery of information. They do not need someone to shepherd their behavior as a parent to a child. Our community does not need an overseer, teacher, director, steering committee or any sort of manipulative leadership; we have Allah as our reality.

Our community must be a living organism. Just as the human body that depends on organs for life, we must continue to develop organizations that function within our community to establish community life that identify us as a body of knowledge founded in the Tafsir of Imam Mohammed.

We should become a member of or assist one or more of the existing organizations. They range from Muslim League of Voters to Muslim Businessmen Association. There are education and inter-faith groups formed in and by our community. They can be associations, corporations or any social, political or economical group in our community concept. We can be a helper in any of them that suit our fancy; "Like minds must come together," as Imam Mohammed pointed out.

In the event, we do not find one that fits our particular interest, we can form one. We should engage others with the same or similar interest, and form an organization to achieve our goal. They should be well structured with chairpersons, presidents, secretaries, sub-committees or any office necessary to complete its task. We need hundreds of such organizations. We need only to remember that Allah supports all good ideas, and move head on into our task. Lastly, as a rule, we should enthusiastically support every organization in our community with our money, time and expertise. We must have faith in Allah and each other. This structure will stabilize our community life in the world.

The exception to this rule should be to withhold our support from any person or organization seeking the power to control our community by dissolving or attempting to reverse our autonomy; or their goals and objectives are clearly against the spirit and letter of Qur'an, life example of Prophet Muhammed (PBUH), insight (Tafsir) of Imam Mohammed or our goals and interests as expressed by the general or majority opinion of our community.

Spirit of Bilal

CHAPTER 21

HAVING A Common PURPOSE

Allah raised Imam Mohammed as his witness and hand to give birth to the community that would follow His word and be a witness and light for the secular world. He was not just concerned with his immediate African-American Muslim Community or the broader African-American community.

He expressed his concern in these words, "We want to make it very clear to you what this mission is all about. We are here to Remake the World, not just the world of mosques, but the World of America and the World outside of America." In these powerful words, he asks us to grab hold to a lofty ambition as well connecting us to a universal destiny.

The world must improve and reverse the negative growth in human behavior that corrupted the society. The key to this change is accepting and establishing our Moral Consciousness as an individual and a society; we must focus on and strive for Human Excellence.

This is a challenge that the world must face. The power is in each human being to meet the test. We must inform the world that Human Excellence is the pattern on which the human being was created; it is the solution for change.

This is the same invitation that Allah sent to human society by way of messengers and prophets—the call for humanity to return to the original pattern which is created in every human being from the beginning. It is our true nature—the original nature of humanity. It can be achieved by having the courage to follow our Moral Conscience for a better world.

The scripture calls this community nature Adam—the perfect man. It is the pattern that will guide the human being to build a better society. Imam Mohammed refers to it as community dynamics as he says, "What is community dynamics? Community dynamics is the interaction of social interest, moral interest, political interest, industrial interest. When all of these interact, they produce a movement. That movement goes forward, as long as human essence is alive in the mix." This emphasizes the importance of Human salvation being at the root of every religious community.

Over the years, and byway of human error instigated by ignorance, greed, lust for power and bad influences, we built a world filled with many inhuman negative qualities. As early societies strayed away from the original pattern, the need for human salvation became more obvious. Putting the society back on the track of human excellence was the main task and purpose of the balanced community formed 1,400 years ago by Prophet Muhammed (PBUH); he followed the lead of Abraham, Moses and Jesus—he was the seal of the Prophets.

Within 1,000 years, this message was buried in human error as the followers gave way to pressures of the characteristics of the secular world; however, all was not lost. The direction and description of the original pattern is still in the Torah, Bible, Qur'an and life example of Prophet Muhammed (PBUH).

Today, we are faced with a world that must change, but it can only be done by those who have the character and "will" of people such as Sampson, Moses, Jesus, Job, John Brown, Booker T. Washington, Clara Muhammad, Prophet Muhammed (PBUH) and hundreds of others who devoted their lives to change. To follow the crowd is an easy proposition, however, to change its direction requires courage, a great deal of courage—Moral Courage.

Commitment is the key ingredient we must have in order to spark the society to employ moral courage for the purpose of building a better society. We must have the kind of commitment of Ibrahiim (Abraham) as he said, "My life and my death are all for Allah." The type of life and death means that our life is devoted to human salvation; and to do that, we are willing to give up weak behavior such as racism, false pride, false concepts, gambling, adultery, lying and adapting the ways of the secular world that will change our message. It will take this kind of commitment to stand up for all human beings working together for better society rather than destroying each other.

The call to human excellence is an invitation that asks all human beings to follow their Moral Conscience and trust that the Creator fashioned every human being with this power for change. Moral Courage will help us to perform our duty as the community calling the world to follow the innate pattern of human excellence. We must not make the same mistakes that were made by the other religious communities; namely, the Israelite, Christian and Muslim. They selected or were abducted by worldly leadership structures that caused them to abandon or at the very least to sway from the purpose that Allah assigned to them.

As a proactive Ummah, conscious of this purpose, our efforts will be the foundation for the new world. The common destiny that Allah revealed in scripture is our invitation to the world; human salvation is the order of the Day, and Human Excellence is our goal.

To our benefit, we have the clear vision given to us by Imam Mohammed to understand the Qur'an and life example of Prophet Mohammed. This is our staff that we have to guide us on this journey.

The prophecy has been fulfilled; a virgin has given birth to a child. Our Community is that child—the Ummah of Imam Mohammed.

The Qur'an says, "He shall speak to the people in childhood and in maturity and he shall be (of the company) of the righteous." The "He" is a new religious community; the Arabic word "Mahdi" in this Ayah is translated as childhood or cradle. In essence, in comparison to all the other religious communities that are hundreds of years old, we are a new community of light that has come into existence; while it is still in its beginning or infancy, it will enlighten humanity of the original purpose Allah intended for the human being.

With the Imam's Tafsir, by the help of Allah, we can understand the prophetic significance of religious text; this is the edification that the world does not have; they have been waiting for it to come. We are that

275

community, the one whose coming has been anticipated for thousands of year, The Body Christ. This great understanding was to come at the end of the time of the old world (ideology), and at the beginning of the new one based on human excellence.

In Suurah Ibrahiim in Ayah 48 when Allah says, "One day the Earth will be changed to a different Earth and so will be the Heavens and (men) will be marshalled forth before Allah the One, the Irresistible." This interprets as to mean that the impact of this new language will produce a new and improved state of mind and condition in the people.

"When you have a vision," says Imam Mohammed, "and you have destiny, you keep your eye on your vision and your destiny." Additionally, he said, "The Body Christ is a congregation of people that will move as Christ, or as one man." He continued, "Christ is the sign of the arrival of spiritual maturity."

He wanted the world to know exactly what Allah had done for us as he said, "We came from slavery, we came from captured life, we came from a position of subhuman, and we shouldn't let ourselves live in this world without wanting to rise up and let the world see we have made it by ourselves."

Our community is highly visible...we are in America, for all eyes to see and all ears to here. Our written and spoken words are being recorded, examined and evaluated by many people outside of our community. They feel our innocence; Allah's word by way of Imam Mohammed's Tafsir is coming through that innocence; we have the power and permission to bring concepts to life. One of those concepts is "IMAM" which most people translate as a leader of men or people, rather than a leader in the "MIND." We caught the hint, when Imam Mohammed said, "Man Means Mind."

Spirit of Bilal

CHAPTER 22

POINTING THE WAY

Allah said to Abraham, "I will make thee an **_Imam_** to the nations (linnaasi)." This episode happened after Abraham had demonstrated his devotion and obedience to Allah.

Abraham was willing to sacrifice the life of his son for the sake his Lord. Then he was stopped and told that he did not have go through with it, because blood did not reach Allah, only obedience reaches Him. The Qur'an says, "And remember that Abraham was tried by his Lord with certain commands which he fulfilled." It was after this situation that Allah called Abraham an Imam. Abraham pleaded for his offspring's to be the same. Allah answered with, "But my promise is not within the reach of evil-doers." This is a clear indication that blood (biological connection), social status or automatic traditions had nothing to do with an Imam. Also, by saying that His promise is not for the evil-doers, establishes that this about the willingness in people to be righteous in their behavior. Right conduct or behavior has its origin in the Moral Conscience—the sense of right and wrong.

Another hint from Qur'an is in the root meaning of the word itself. Imam is a word that is root in the same "MM" as is Ummi (mother) and Ummah (community); they all are connected the root "umm." Most important, they are connected in terms of function. Imam (leader) comes out of the Ummah (community) that he leads. Ummi (mother) is the first teacher of the child that becomes the community. In fact, Prophet Muhammad is called the Ummi Prophet by Allah in the Qur'an.

This suggests that in some form, Imam is rooted in primal origin of the original creation. Also, it is an indication that everyone is connected to the same origin because they came from Adam.

As a community finding our place in the scheme of things, we are faced with this metaphor that is a symbol of something greater than the obvious. It is the way the word "Imam" is used rather than what it implies; understanding this concept, is at the core of our purpose.

Imam means leader; the one who stands in front. Like many other concepts, there is an explicit and implicit understanding of this meaning.

The explicit or obvious understanding addresses the religious leader of Muslim communities throughout the world. Additionally, there are certain duties expected of his position that adds the meaning of what is an Imam.

The Imam must be a male over a community of believers, especially a mixed congregation of male and female. He must be a Muslim of high standard of piety, character, knowledge, and a desire to have complete obedience to Allah. He must teach the community how to apply the religion in everyday life, promote Islamic Knowledge through education to the best of his ability. He should be available to provide counseling, perform Jumuah prayers, Eid prayers, Tarweed and five daily prayers (Fajr, Dhuhr, Asa, Mahgrib and Isha'a). He must perform weddings and Janazah prayers (funerals). Ironically, these duties do not separate or make him special because these characteristics that are expected of every Muslim.

The average believer, especially male, is expected to be able to perform these duties and have the same characteristic, particularly if he is the head of the household in the Muslim family. By the time a male child reaches twelve, he is expected to begin performing these practices. There are no procedures or qualifications other than aforementioned expectations to be an Imam.

Furthermore, each community (Ummah) is autonomous; therefore, any Muslim community can select whoever they choose to serve as Imam of that community; of course, piety of character should be the first and main quality of the one they choose; nevertheless, the choice is theirs. In fact, no one can assume or be place in the role over an Ummah as an Imam against the will of the community; it must be the choice of the community (congregation) which is the only certification for the position. It should be someone from their immediate congregation.

The process is very simple because there is no hierarchy or priesthood in Al-Islam; it is one Ummah and everyone is equal. Therefore, because the term receives such an honorable and elevated status in the Qur'an, there must be a greater meaning and purpose of the term Imam—an implicit meaning or understanding that is deserving of such an eminent position.

While the term Imam is used several times in the Qur'an, seldom does it deal with this concept as an administrative position. Neither does it suggest duties nor definitions of responsibilities. It addresses something that goes first or in front, but it is not a person. It distinguishes the characteristic from the character.

For example; the following Ayah will highlight Imam with squares to identify it from the rest of the text. Furthermore, the underlines are not in the original quotes; for our purpose, it is easier to identify specific aspects while we are examining them. In addition to the transliteration, Yusuf Ali and Mohammad M. Pickthall are the two English translations of them.

Suratul Al Israa 17: Ayah 71

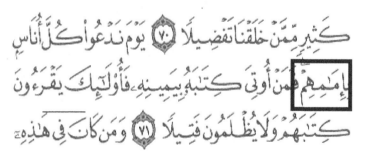

Ali: "One day We shall call together all human beings with their (respective) *Imams:* those who are given their record in their right hand will read it (with pleasure) and they will not be dealt with unjustly in the least."

Pickthall: "On the day when We shall summon all men with their _record_, whoso is given his book in his right hand such will read their book and they will not be wronged a shred."

TransliterationYawma nad-'uu kulla 'unaasim-bi-**_Imaamihim_**: faman 'uutiya kitaabahuu bi-yamihii fa-'ulaa-'ola uaqra 'uun kitaabahum wa laa yuz-lamuuna fatiilaa.

In this first example, firstly, it is clear that Imam is in the Arabic text. Secondly, and just as clear, both scholars define the word Imam differently. Ali sticks with literal term Imam; however, he preceded it with the word respective. Respective means own, personal or individual. It appears as if he is indicating that everyone has their own Imam that will witness for or against them on Judgment Day. On the other hand, Pickthall defines Imam as a record that contains everything. It too will witness for or against the individual. How they treat the next Ayat is just as diverse.

Surutul Huud 11: Ayah 17

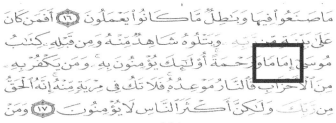

Ali: "Can they be (like) those who accept a Clear (Sign) from their Lord and whom a witness from Himself doth teach as did the Book of Moses before it *a guide* and a mercy? They believe therein; but those of the Sects that reject it the Fire will be their promised meeting place. Be not then in doubt thereon: for it is the Truth from thy Lord: yet many among men do not believe!"

Pickthall: "Is he (to be counted equal with them) who relieth on a clear proof from his Lord, and a witness from Him reciteth it, and before it was the Book of Moses, *an example* and a mercy? Such believe therein, and Whoso disbelieveth therein of the clans, the Fire is his appointed place. So be not thou in doubt concerning it. Lo! it is the Truth from thy Lord; but most of mankind believe not."

TransliterationAfaman ka_na 'ala_ bayyinatim mir rabbihi wa yatlu_hu sya_hidum minhu wa min rabbihi kita_ba mu_sa_ *imaam*aw wa rahmah (tan), ula-'ika yu'minu_na bih(i), wa may yakfur bihi minal ahza_bi fan na_ru mau'iduhu_ fala_ taku fi miryatim minhu innahul haqqu mir rabbika wa la_kinna aksaran na_si la_ yu'minu_n(a).

As in the first example, the Arabic word Imam is clearly in the Ayah, but this time, it is identifying purpose of the Book of Moses which is the same as the witness who

285

came with the same information. However, again, both men treat it different. Ali uses 'a guide' to make his point—while Pickthall prefers 'an example.' Although, both words are directive, a guide can steer which is different from illustration, model or pattern which refer to an example. However, the problem with the two men is not so much with the choice of English words they used to express their point of view; the problem is that they both show inconsistencies in their approach and observation with Imam. This holds true in our final Ayah that uses the Arabic Imam as it relates to the Believers.

Al Baqarah 124

Ali: "And remember that Abraham was tried by his Lord with certain commands which he fulfilled; He said: "I will make thee an _**Imam**_ to the nations." He pleaded: "And also (Imams) from my offspring!"   He answered: "But my promise is not within the reach of evil-doers."

Pickthall: "And (remember) when his Lord tried Abraham with (His) commands, and he fulfilled them, He said: Lo! I have appointed thee *a leader* for mankind. (Abraham) said: And of my offspring (will there be leaders)? He said: My covenant includeth not wrongdoers."

TransliterationWa izibtala_ ibra_hima rabbuhu_ bi kalima_tin fa atammahunn (a), qa_la inni ja_'iluka linna_si *ima ma* (n), qa_la wa min zurriyyati, qa_la la_ yana_lu 'ahdiz za_limin(a).

Ali goes back to using Imam to define Imam; however, in this case, he uses nation for the word naasi which makes Imam more of a states-man or political position in terms of status. Whereas, **Pickthall** uses mankind for naasi; he uses the word leader for Imam. Because nation is defined as country, homeland, state and sometimes population, and mankind is viewed as civilization, humanity or even people, it seems as though they used the English out of place. Imam is better with mankind, and leader is better with nation. This only emphasizes the importance of reading Qur'an for ourselves.

When we examine word Imam and how it is used in the Qur'an, and with Tafsir of Imam Mohammed to assist us in making important connections, we will find that there is a deeper and implicit meaning to this term.

For instance, in the case (respective) Imam and record, which ever term is used, it is something or someone that would have to be with us all the time even from our birth or our acceptance of the religion; it is personal.

It cannot be identifying the Imam of Masajid or Islamic Centers; they cannot follow and record the activities of every member of the congregation on a daily or minute by minute basis even as it relates to just religious activities. Furthermore, they were not with us since our birth; it is farfetched to consider such a thing. The feasibility of such a task is not in the realm of reality.

Subsequently, in reality, comprehending this concept requires the use of our rational approach to follow this idea of Imam to its logical conclusion.

As you study the Qur'an, you will find that there is another ingredient that makes up this natural package to form the Moral Conscience; it is Taqwá (original fear). It is the combination between the Nafs (soul) and Taqwá that gives birth to the Moral Conscience in each of us for moral guidance. This is the natural instinct that stimulates our drive for righteousness; it is the mother that receives this package first in her child. She prepares it for the community. And in return, the community prepares it for world leadership.

As the most valuable role in the human family, the mother takes that soul as a baby and begins teaching it morals from her own nature and instincts. That is the life that Allah entrusted her with. She must teach the moral life to the child as it is maturing. She establishes in the mind of the child a sense of right and wrong that in most cases is compatible with that which is created in its nature. This is the basis of its moral life that will mature into the lead component in each human being that the Qur'an identifies as Imam.

Your Imam began in you at conception and grew while you are still a baby. Allah created it in your soul in the form of taqwa. This is the course of development of every human being regardless of sex, ethnicity, race or nationality.

Our understanding about this concept of Imam is the key. Our purpose is to deliver the correct picture to the world in order that they may grasp this vital aspect of human excellence. Their human growth hinges on this factor.

To present Imam as a concept, with little distortion as possible, we must be clear about this expression. This word is as important to our mission as fuel is to powerful engines used to transform raw materials into useful products. It is the catalyst for the new world.

Because Imam must be with all of us for our entire lives, and innocent and obedient to Allah, it is clear that the word is symbolic to the greatest force in the human being, the "Moral Conscience." Therefore, Imam is a concept word that stands for the Moral Conscience in every human being.

CHAPTER 23

CALLING

Every individual, family, community, society, civilization or social group has either principles, ethics or sense of right and wrong that governs its behavior—Moral Conscience. It is the Moral Conscience that Allah asks us to follow; it has been with the human being as a guide since the beginning of time. We must call the world to get back on the path of human excellence by focusing on this aspect of our original nature.

Over the years, different people and ideologies, in an attempt to control humanity, distorted and in some cases destroyed the Moral Consciousness in the society. Then, they would replace it with their philosophy as a guide for humanity. This action by the human being is the portion of man that Allah refers to as Satan or Shaitan. It also occurs daily in individuals.

For example, when a person makes a decision or chooses to do something for the sake of money, power, greed, lust, or anything that is against what their Moral Conscience suggests to them at first glance this is how human being begin to evolve into Satan. This pattern is revealed is many places in the scriptures.

The story of Jesus' crucifixion is not about the death of a man; it is about a group in the society that distorted or killed the Moral Conscience in the people in order to control them. Jesus is the symbol for the Moral Conscience in humanity. There is the story of Jacob and his mother (community) that deceived Isaac (correct Knowledge) his father to gain the birth right over his older brother Ezra (Moral Conscious community). Cain (Desire to rule) killing Abel (Moral Conscience) is another story. Joseph's (Moral Conscience) brother dropping him in a deep hole, leaving him to die, is still another. When your eyes open, you can see these stories and many more throughout scripture that depict acts of treachery in human society are the evolution of Satan, and the Crucifixion of the Moral Conscience in humanity.

The story and idea in scripture of a "chosen people" or "messiah" should be viewed as something other than just about physical people. It was about the fact that Allah chose the Moral Conscience in every human being to lead and build human society. It is byway of the Moral Conscience that Allah guides humanity; it is not by the "blood."

Furthermore, you will find that there is an underlining factor that addresses the redemption or resurrection of the Moral Conscience, especially, in the last day of the world of falsehood.

In these, the last days, Allah will raise up the Moral Conscience in humanity all over the world. Even in the most primitive or sophisticated cultures, the Moral Conscience is being raised to place humanity back on the path of human excellence. We, the community and others like us, were brought into existence to call the world to this beautiful event. We must encourage them to use the power of the Moral Conscience that Allah has in them. We are in the day when the path to human excellence will be filled with those who have the "moral courage" to follow their Moral Conscience. They will put down their labels and pickup From that time forth began Jesus to show unto his disciples, the banner of human salvation. Even those such as liars, murders, thieves, corrupters of truth who may be considered as having no morals and deviants in the society will change; the defeated, tormented, or victimized Moral Conscience in them will rise and take its place to lead them to help build a better society; a society where human life is more important than inanimate objects or the desire to overtly or covertly control others for personal gain. The only requirement in such a society is that every human being follows their Moral Conscience.

1,400 years ago, Prophet Muhammed (PBUH) established a community on the basis of the Qur'an. He left many examples to serve as a guide for humanity. One of the most powerful and expressing all details in a clear and obvious way, leaving no doubt as to the intended meaning was congregational salah (prayer).

For the Muslim participant, it addresses an order and conformation to leadership. As to the observer, the conclusion is the same.

When two or more Muslims pray together, one must lead and the others follow his movements. Therefore, including in a congregation, the one that stands in front and lead the rest in prayer is the Imam (leader in prayer); the others follow his lead. They listen to and follow silently what he says except in two procedures.

The first place occurs as the Imam rises from the position called Ar-Ruku (bowing), he says, "Sami Allahu li man hami-dah." This means that Allah listens to all who praise him. The congregation rises and says, "Rabba na la ka-l-hamd." This means that Our Lord to Thee is due all praise. The second place is at the conclusion while everyone is the position of Al Jalsa (sitting position). The Imam turns his head to the right and says, "As-Salamu 'alai-kum wa rahmatu llah." This means Peace be on you and the mercy of Allah. Then, he turns his head to the left and repeats the same phase. Following him, the congregation does and says the same procedure. The Imam is generally selected by those who follow him. This method was established by Prophet Muhammed (PBUH).

Understanding the view that Imam is symbolic for the Moral Conscience in the human being, this thought out and purposely arranged procedure has two very important and practical meanings.

First, the individual who leads and those who follow the prayer are demonstrating submission and commitment to follow their Moral Conscience over and above their intellect and emotions as the leader in their spiritual makeup. Subsequently, each individual will conduct and govern their daily behavior in the manner that reflects the agreement. Allah guides the human being as long as they follow their Moral Conscience.

Second, the congregation illustrates a hope and sign for the leaders in the secular society to follow their Moral Conscience to guide them in their political, economical, educational and religious interests. This is the proper meaning of leadership.

All subsequent prayers are a reminder and recommitment of these two very important meanings of the performance of prayer.

We are thankful to Allah for His Messenger, Prophet Muhammed (PBUH). As the Messenger of Allah, he has been a great example for humanity especially as he demonstrated the practical application of the Qur'an. Additionally, we do not want to be remised in our acknowledgement of the other great Messengers who Allah Blessed humanity with such as Jesus, Moses and many others. The same message we find in the Qur'an about the Moral Conscience was brought by them in the books they received from Allah for humanity.

For example the Jews, they read and followed the Torah. The Torah is filled with a succession of prophets and messengers who had a direct influence on the religious community. Each of them clearly stated that they were from the Creator and Lord of all things, especially the Jews. Each of them established clear direction for them to follow.

While they were symbols of the Moral Conscience and addressed the morality of the people, the succession concluded with Moses; it was Moses who illuminated any doubt regarding the moral standards in the people. Allah gave him the Law (Mosaic Laws) that established the importance of the Moral Conscience in the people. This is the same Moral Conscience expressed in the Qur'an, and the words of Jesus that followed Moses.

Jesus in the book of Matthew 5:17-18 of the Bible, as he stated, "Think not that I am come to destroy the law, or the prophets: I am not come to destroy, but to fulfill. For verily I say unto you, Till heaven and earth pass, one jot or one title shall in no wise pass from the law, till all be fulfilled." In modern terms, as Jesus uses the jot (atom), he is clear about the importance the fact that he said that he is the fulfillment of the law. He established that the law is the building block and basis for human excellence byway of the Moral Conscience; he is symbolic of the Moral Conscience.

He continued the point in St. John as he depicts the Moral Conscience as a door. In 10:1, he says, "Verily, verily, I say unto you, He that entereth not by the door into the sheepfold, but climbeth up some other way, the same is a thief and a robber." Understanding the Tafsir of Imam Mohammed, it is reasonable to figure that Jesus identifies the door as the Moral Conscience or good intention in the human being as the right character for leadership; the term for that in Arabic is Bashir; the sheep represents good people. Therefore, any leader that approaches good people by any other means than their Moral Conscience guiding them, has bad intention for the people, and will rob good or righteous people of their money, power, time and life. Directing our attention to the value of the Moral Conscience, Jesus, in 10:2, says, "But he that entereth in by the door is the shepherd of the sheep." Here, it is without doubt that Jesus is pointing out that leadership who comes with Moral Conscience as their leader means well for the people and will serve them well.

Nearly every Christian must agree that Jesus placed the entire qualification to enter the kingdom of heaven on the importance of the Moral Conscience. He defined himself as the embodiment of Moral Conscience when in 10:9-10 he said, "I am the door: by me if any man enters in, he shall be saved, and shall go in and out, and find pasture." Pasture represents a good and honest life. Jesus continued, "The thief cometh not, but for to steal, and to kill, and to destroy: I am come that they might have life, and that they might have it more abundantly." Need anymore be said about good leadership? It is Jesus' entire mission that addressed the value of Moral Conscience in the human family, and he was a symbol of the leadership (Moral Conscience) in each of us. He concludes this argument in 10:6, as he says, "I am the way, the truth, and the life: no man cometh unto the Father, but by me." The profundity of the statement is in the form of a commandment, perhaps the most important of all commandments—it orders or instructs that we must live with our Moral Conscience as the first principle in our life because it is the only way to please Allah.

Allah created the conscious mind with its intellect to engage the creation, an emotional component for stimulation and appreciation, and a soul (Nafs) for moral guidance. The soul was created with a conscience—a sense of what is wrong and right for it.

We have been formed for the expressed purpose to usher in the new world led by the Moral Conscience striving for human excellence—a world that hold human salvation above everything else.

This is why it is of grave importance and incumbent on our community to bring the religious and secular world's attention to the works and insight of Imam Mohammed.

This must be reflected in everything we produce such as books, poems, blog, letters and news articles to benefit the society at-large. Along with news print, speakers and lecturers must address the outside community way of this language. Others can form small interfaith groups to study together. Individuals can participate in one on one discussion.

In the midst of the complexities of the world, with the Spirit of Bilal, we must stand on the side of truth and righteousness, but we must also commit ourselves unconditionally to call them to "Human Excellence" through this language. For the pleasure of Allah, we promote the Moral Conscience in everyone regardless of their race, sex, religion, political views or position in the society.

On October 5, 2007, Friday Asr prayer in Ramadan Session, Imam Mohammed stated, "Bilal, may Allah be pleased with him, there is a lot in Bilal that you do not know. Only a few of you know. Bilal is a prophetic picture and I do not mean a prophet." Making the distinction for his listeners, he continued, "Prophetic picture does not mean, necessarily, a prophet, but it means a picture out of prophecy." To highlight this issue, the Imam explained, "He is a picture that we can find in Bible prophecy and writings." Ordinarily, the story about Bilal stems from Hadith.

Imam Mohammed concluded his remarks concerning Bilal as he said, "He is not there by accident as the Mu'adhan for Prophet Muhammed." Summarizing the focus on Bilal is not one we should take lightly. It is a captivating explanation of the connection all scripture and people. Allah has raised the Moral Conscience in humanity for righteousness, high principles of conduct, excellence in character, and dignity to lift humanity above petty, unclean, and ignorant behavior. With truth and understanding, we must be a voice for human salvation by encouraging humanity to strive for Human Excellence.

Spirit of Bilal

HOLY QUR'AN
SURATAH 'ALAQ (THE CLOT) NO. 96
(VERSES 1-5)
WITH THE NAME OF ALLAH, THE BENEFICENT, THE MERCIFUL

1. Read (Proclaim!) In the Name of your Lord who created
2. Created man, out of a clot (of congealed blood).
3. Read (Proclaim), and your Lord is the Most Generous,
4. Who taught by the Pen,
5. Taught man that which he knew not.

KING JAMES VERSION OF BIBLE: GENESIS 2:7

"And the LORD God formed man of the dust of the ground, and breathed into his nostrils the breath of life: and man became a living soul."

Made in the USA
Las Vegas, NV
11 March 2021